GW00402482

CRAFTY IDEAS

The authors are sisters and teach in primary schools in Leeds and Hull. They have published a children's story book and **Myrna Daitz** contributes articles to *Nursery World.*

CRAFTY IDEAS

Myrna Daitz & Shirley Williams

With illustrations by Annie Tomlin

SEVERN
HOUSE

Our thanks go to all the children whose
enquiring minds and intelligent questions
gave birth to this book.

Our special thanks go to Lesley Menzer
whose original drawings have been
invaluable in conceiving and planning
the final artwork in this book.

M.D. & S.W.

British Library Cataloguing in Publication Data
Daitz, Myrna
    Crafty ideas.
    1. Handicraft — Juvenile literature
    I. Title   II. Williams, Shirley
    680'24054   TT160
    ISBN 0-7278-2009-5

Published by Severn House Publishers Limited
144-146 New Bond Street
London W1Y 9FD

Text ©Myrna Daitz and Shirley Williams 1981
Illustrations ©Severn House Publishers Limited

Editorial: **Ian Jackson**
Design: **Rob Burt**

Colour separation by Culver Graphics Litho Ltd,
High Wycombe, Buckinghamshire
Typesetting by TJB Photosetting Ltd,
South Witham, Lincolnshire
Printed and bound by Grafichromo, S.A.,
Cordoba, Spain

Contents

Introduction

At the present time more than any other, parents are anxious to involve themselves with their children's education. However interested parents are, they have not been trained as teachers have to understand the educational concepts by which the children are taught each subject every day. Many parents enjoy making things with their young children, but the educational value of their cutting and pasting is rarely appreciated. We feel the time has come for a book to be written which not only presents a wide range of interesting projects for young children to make at home (or school) with or without supervision, but which also helps *parents* to understand and appreciate the reasons behind the craft work taught in schools. We both teach in primary schools and for some time we have realised that there is a need for a fresh approach to craft work at home for young children. We feel strongly that the educational value of craft work has been very much under emphasised and few books have been published which show both interesting and exciting hand work for children and also provide the educational back up. With the modern educational practice of 'learning through doing' being taught in training colleges today, craft work with children is entering a new era.

Each item presented here has an educational value as well as being fun to make, and once you are aware of the possibilities, you can extend the concepts into everything you do with your child. When your child brings home a piece of work he has made in a craft lesson at school, you will admire it but the chances are it will soon be thrown away. Before you finally discard it, let us tell you exactly what the child achieved while he was working on it. He has completed a lesson in mathematics, an exercise in language development and an extension of his emotional make-up and social behaviour. In fact, this one piece of work represents hours of hard work and forethought by his teacher. The end product for you to see is but a tiny drop in the ocean of your child's education.

The crafty ideas

All the projects in *Crafty Ideas* have been made by the children in the schools in which we teach. Many of them reflect their own original ideas, and others are variations on old themes. They have been made by children of varying ages, and it is interesting to note how different age groups will use the ideas. For example, the younger child of say 3 or 4 years will be satisfied with making the Halloween models. The older child will discover how easy it is to make these basic items and will enlarge upon them, stretch his imagination and develop his use of size, colour and shape. He will discover a larger choice of decorations and produce more sophisticated versions of the same models. He can make his own Halloween party invitations and decorate the room with witches suspended by black cotton threaded through the point of the hat to give a flying effect. Spooky bats or spiders and cats with glittering eyes hanging down from unexpected places can lend atmosphere to his party. The older child can develop the idea of a puppet theatre made from a cardboard carton, and use the models to act out a Halloween play. We want to encourage adaptation and development of the basic ideas by different age groups and this is one of the main concepts of our book. Each model will stimulate the child's imagination and intelligence, allowing him to develop intellectually and emotionally in his own way, and at his own pace.

many of the projects including the **Valentine Card** (page 50), the **Halloween Bat** (page 26) and the **Collage on Polystyrene** (page 60). Using scissors, painting and pasting are all exercises which develop manipulation in young children. This is a very important skill, because the child who cannot easily do these exercises will be hampered at a later date when ease of writing and quickness of thought are useful advantages in his later education and throughout life.

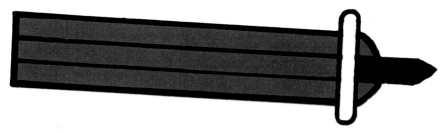

The value of the projects

The items have been chosen to train and develop the different skills which a child must achieve. Classifying objects into sets is the first step towards mathematics, and every opportunity to sort out craft materials should be used to the full. Leaves for the **Real Leaf Picture** (page 18), pasta, straws and felt for **Sets of Shapes** (page 24), tissue paper, bus tickets, and materials for the **Collage on Polystyrene** (page 60) all form basic lessons around this theme. The development of hand and eye coordination comes into play when preparing cones, folding and pleating, and cutting and gluing, all of which are needed in the making of the **Christmas Angel**, the **Three Kings and Mary** and the **Halloween Witch** (pages 40, 42 and 32). Careful measurement and precision work are featured in several items, among them the **Handy Jotter** (page 66), **Circle Quiz** (page 100), **Multi-shaped Clown** (page 22), **Tube Santa** (page 34), **Pressed Flower Book Mark** (page 58), **Easter Basket** (page 78) and **Window Box** (page 90). Colour, shape and symmetry are highlighted in

Handy hints

When your child is ready for a craft session, it is important that you gather together all the items that will be needed, before you start. It is very frustrating to be almost finished and then to find that a vital piece of equipment or material is missing. To help you prepare for each project we have listed everything required in a 'What you need' box. Always cover your working surface with newspapers so that when the project is completed it is easy to gather up all the left over bits and pieces and throw them away. This is also basic training in tidiness for your child. Scissors with rounded ends can be used but we prefer to use small pointed steel scissors, and to train the child from the start to use them correctly and safely. When making a project with a small child, you will need to sit with him to explain and help, but older children will enjoy working out the step-by-step directions themselves, or with a friend.

There are many types of waste materials suitable for project work which can be obtained at little or no cost. Wallpaper shops will often oblige with an outdated sample book. Stores which sell materials often have small sample swatches they will give away, and some sell packets of mixed materials very cheaply. Clothing and seed catalogues are always useful to keep, and birthday and Christmas cards should never be thrown away, as they provide card, pictures and often metallic paper. Most towns have an art and craft shop which sells coloured card, crepe, tissue and gummed papers, and sugar paper which is a coarse textured paper available in several colours. It is important always to ask for non-toxic paints for children's craft work. Rubber-based adhesives and a strong white glue are also obtainable at these shops, and powder paint or poster paints in many colours. Any stationer with a baking accessory department will stock rice paper. A set of felt-tipped pens, coloured wax crayons, pencils and a ruler complete your basic equipment, but remember that almost everything else you need is already in your kitchen cupboard!

large container in which you can keep a collection of junk materials. All household boxes can be used. Milk bottle tops, tins and yoghurt cartons, (previously sterilised), egg boxes, packets and cartons are just some of the materials you will find in your kitchen. Once you realise the potential of an egg box or a toilet roll tube, you and your children can have hours of creative fun. Wallpaper, pieces of polystyrene, newspapers, magazines and even old computer print outs can be used effectively. Making up the models can stimulate the imagination of the entire family, and even Grandma may surprise you with a series of yoghurt carton puppets!

From an educational point of view, a child working at junk modelling explores facts, reasons, judges and draws conclusions. In fact he learns to think. Skill is acquired in the use of scissors and a great deal of concentration is developed when measuring and fitting items together. The child will benefit from the artistic creations he produces and the less artistic child will not be distressed if something does not turn out correctly because failures can be discarded at no cost and started again. Finally, encourage your child to tidy out the junk box regularly for this gives valuable experience in sorting and classifying items.

Conservation lessons

Conservation is a vitally important lesson which we should try to introduce to our children. Children should realise how much we waste and the possible effect this can have on our environment. We feel strongly about this and you will find that most of the items in the book can be made from household materials which you would normally throw away; we have also included a section especially on junk modelling (pages 80 to 100). Try to find a

Fun in the kitchen

Cooking together is great fun for your children and their friends on a rainy day. Gather together all the ingredients required before they begin and cover the kitchen floor with newspapers to make it easier to clear up spills. Aprons should be worn with sleeves well rolled up. Some of the recipes are 'no-bake' requiring no use of hot plate or oven but others need cooking at high temperatures, and we would like to stress the need for strict adult supervision at all times for these particular recipes. Allow your child to complete the early stages, and then to watch this cooking process, which will enable you to emphasise the dangers of boiling oil and hot ovens.

Children begin to identify shapes in the kitchen as they make balls of mixture and roll them out. While the children are beating egg whites for **Crafty Mousse Faces** (page 102), discuss the wonderful change that has taken place from the sloppy, transparent albumen to the mound of stiff, pure white mixture they have produced. Some changes of shape are obviously reversible whereas others are not. Share the mixture as equally as possible and let the children compare size, shape, thickness and length. In this way they are having fun but at the same time assimilating many mathematical concepts. The best tools are hands and fingers and the child will derive deep satisfaction from working with his hands. This is a good opportunity for the parent to talk about the importance of cleanliness to avoid germs and infection. Artistically presented, the **Coconut Barfi** and **Chocolate Biscuit Cakes** make excellent gifts for Christmas, Easter and Mother's and Father's Day. Elsewhere in the book are baskets and containers for the gifts.

Festivals and celebrations

We have discussed at some length the physical and intellectual benefits to be gained from craft work. Equally important however are the emotional and social benefits. Whilst making the items for Christmas or Easter for example, take the opportunity to discuss the traditions and beliefs behind the festivals with your children. This is the perfect opportunity for a parent to enlarge the child's knowledge and vocabulary and to give the older child an introduction to the idea of other religions, races, colours and creeds. This will help to develop a greater understanding between children of different races. Here are a few pointers to possible questions your children may ask together with some useful facts and figures about the festivals for which projects are suggested in the book.

Halloween is the last night in October, and the time of the year when children enjoy frightening each other and themselves by dressing up as witches and warlocks. There are many superstitions connected with Halloween, and in mediaeval times strange rituals took place in order to frighten away witches. Today Halloween is an occasion for fun, games and parties. However, many young children have deep-seated fears of the dark and are upset by ghostly tales, so here is the perfect opportunity for adults to explain some of the myths and legends. When your child has made his very own Halloween models, and listened to several light-hearted stories about witches and ghosts, many of his fears will disappear leaving only the fun.

Thanksgiving Day is an American festival celebrated on the fourth Thursday in November. It is a historical, national and religious holiday that began with the Pilgrims in 1621. The first Thanksgiving ceremony was a three-day festival when the Pilgrims feasted with their Indian guests on wild turkey. Today it is an annual day of thanks for the blessings of the past year. The symbols of Thanksgiving are pumpkin pie and turkey. We suggest you encourage your children to try our **Turkey Tasters** (page 110) to stimulate discussion about this event.

Christmas It is good for a child to learn at an early age that Christmas is not just about receiving presents and that in addition to the religious significance it is an opportunity to make gifts to give to others. Although he will be busy at school doing craft work, this is your opportunity to work closely with your child to decorate your home instead of buying commercial decorations.

Chanukah is a Jewish festival lasting for eight days, which usually occurs very near to Christmas. It commemorates the Maccabean revolt of 165 BCE (Before the Christian Era), when a small group of Jews led by the famous Judas Maccabeus won an important battle against the Assyrian-Greek army. Legend tells that the Temple had been defiled by the enemy and had to be reconsecrated. However when the Jews relit the lamp in the temple, the oil they had left was sufficient only for one day. Miraculously, the oil lasted for the eight days it took to prepare new holy oil. Today all over the world Jewish people celebrate the festival of Chanukah for eight days by lighting a Menorah (page 48) which is an eight-branched candlestick, and adding an additional candle each day. Presents are exchanged at this time and some families have the pleasant custom of giving a small present each night so as to increase the enjoyment of the festival.

St Valentine's Day has grown very popular in England. Valentine was a priest who lived in Rome in the third century AD and was beheaded for giving shelter to Christians. At about the same time the Romans celebrated a Pagan festival of 'Love Feasts and Lotteries' when it was the custom for all the teenage boys and girls to draw slips of paper from an urn, and to keep company with the person whose name they had drawn. Later the church dedicated the 'Love Feasts and Lotteries' to Saint Valentine, who really had nothing to do with it at all. Valentine verses were written in Shakespeare's time, and by the beginning of the nineteenth century cards were being printed. Today we send cards and gifts to people we love and this is a very enjoyable custom.

Mother's and Father's Day Many of our traditions are based on myths and legends from Pagan times and it is thought that Mothering Sunday is based on the story of a goddess called Cybele. She was worshipped as the mother of the gods but with the advent of Christianity the story was adapted and the date used for a different purpose. Mothering Sunday is the fourth Sunday in Lent and, in the more recent past, became the time when young apprentices and servants were allowed the day home from work in order to visit their mothers. These boys and girls would take flowers, gifts or cakes and the special Simnel cakes which are still baked today.

Father's Day originated in the United States and is celebrated there and in Great Britain on the third Sunday in June. The idea was originated by Mrs John Bruce Dodd who in 1909 persuaded the ministers of Spokane Wash to salute fathers with special church services. The idea was officially approved by President Woodrow Wilson in 1916. Later, President Calvin Coolidge recommended National Observance for the occasion, 'to establish more intimate relations between fathers and their children, and to impress upon fathers the full measure of their obligations'. In England we celebrate Father's Day by sending cards and giving presents.

Easter sometimes comes in March and sometimes in April and an enquiring child may ask the reason why their birthday fell at Easter last year and not this year. The date of Easter was decided many centuries ago as the first Sunday following the first full moon after the spring equinox. Equinox is the time of year when the sun crosses the Equator and day and night become equal in length. The custom of making and giving Easter eggs is a fitting association with spring. Eggs symbolize the beginning of new life and chocolate Easter eggs are a modern development of a very old custom of giving eggs as spring gifts.

The Fourth of July is an important and exciting day for Americans. It is one of the chief legal holidays of the United States and commemorates the formal adoption of the Declaration of American Independence in 1776. In the early days the holiday had a formal religious tone but nowadays parades, outings and sports are all a part of the celebrations. Let your children make **Uncle Sam's Banana Whizz** (page 106) and **Salami Surprises** (page 114).

Drawing with the templates

Children love drawing but there are times when they are dissatisfied with their efforts because, unless they are extremely artistically gifted, young children cannot produce on paper the picture which they have in their mind. To help overcome this, we have provided several attractive drawings in the final section which the children can copy to make templates. Drawing round the templates gives outlines which can be used for so many different ideas. Pencil holders and gift containers can be made when an outline produced from a template is attached to a painted toilet roll tube for example. Calendars and cards for all occasions and a colourful bedroom wall frieze and various mobiles all stem from the basic

templates. By using the grid method explained on page 116, the outlines provided can be accurately copied onto a piece of card, cut out and used as templates. The children can then colour and decorate their pictures in their own individual way.

Finally

We hope that this book will open your eyes to the endless possibilities of extending your child's abilities, language and knowledge, and that you will become aware that everything you do together can be used to further his or her education. An autumn walk with the family for example provides an opportunity to search for all the free craft material that nature donates to us at this time of year. Conkers from the horse chestnut tree, pine cones, leaves, twigs and the many plants and flowers which can be dried to use for decorations are all readily available. A trip to the coast can produce a variety of shells, feathers and interesting stones, all of which can be stored away for future craft work.

We hope that you will enjoy and appreciate the educational value of the projects in the following pages, have fun working with your child and that this book will give you a deeper insight and understanding of the modern concept of 'learning through doing'.

...and Tree

How to make it

1. Draw and cut a tree shape about 45 cm high from sugar paper. Paint it brown.
2. Draw round your hand on pieces of thin card. Draw round the hands of other people.
3. Cut out the hand shapes.
4. Colour the hand shapes with paints or crayons.
5. Glue the hand shapes on to the branches and display the tree on a wall.

1

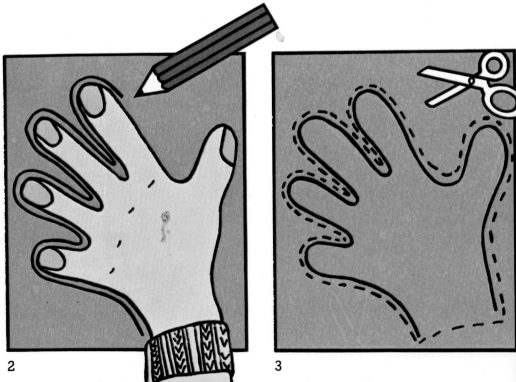

2

3

What you need
Sugar paper
Pencil
Scissors
Card
Paints or crayons
Glue

Parent's handy hint
Encourage your child to draw round his hand from left to right. This will help his writing ability.

4

5

Real Leaf Picture

1

How to make it

1   Have ready a selection of leaves and twigs.
2   For each picture use a piece of stiff card approximately 20 cm x 30 cm.
3   Using a twig as a centre-piece glue it on using strong glue.
4   Arrange the leaves in a pleasing manner around the twig and glue them in position.
5   When dry paint with colourless varnish.
6   Using gummed paper or coloured sellotape make a contrasting frame for the picture.

2

3

4

What you need
Leaves and twigs
Stiff card
Glue
Clear varnish
Gummed paper or
coloured sellotape

Parent's handy hint
Collecting the leaves and
twigs can make an interesting project for a family
outing. The picture can
be used as a calendar or
as a hanging picture.

5

6

Cheese Carton Plaque

How to make it

1 Take a cheese carton and trim the edge of the lid with pinking shears. Paint the inside and outside a bright colour.

2 Cut a circle of white paper to fit inside the lid.

3 Fold the circle in half and then in half again. Make small cuts along the folded edges and cut out different shapes from the centre. The more cuts made, the prettier the end result.

4/5 Open out the doiley and colour with paints or crayon. Glue a piece of coloured tape to the top of the carton.

6 Glue the doiley into the carton and decorate with leaves and twigs glued on firmly.

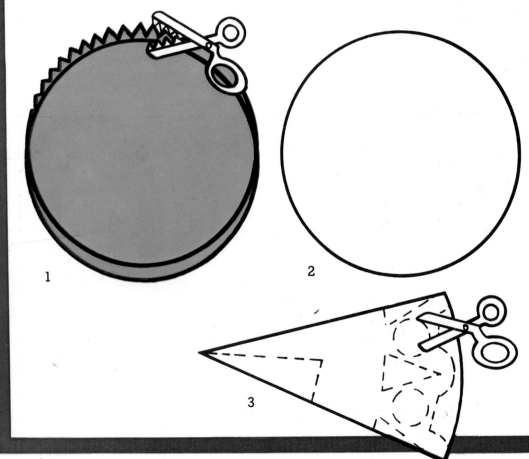

4

What you need
Cheese carton
Pinking shears
Paints or crayons
White paper
Scissors
Glue
Leaves and twigs

Parent's handy hint
Help may be needed in
cutting out the folded
doiley. Can be used as a
wine glass coaster, a gift
for various occasions, or
as a calendar if holly leaves
with berries are
substituted.

5

6

Multi-shape Clown

How to make it

1 Cut a rectangle approximately 12 cm x 8 cm from stiff card for the body and colour with stripes.

2 Cut four strips approximately 25 cm x 4 cm for legs and arms and colour.

3 Cut a triangle with approximately 8 cm sides for the hat and colour.

4 Cut a circle approximately 8 cm across for the face.

5 Fold the legs and arms in a concertina fashion.

6 Draw and colour the face, or use gummed papers for the features.

7 Dip cotton wool balls into dry powder paint to make buttons. Shake and glue to the body.

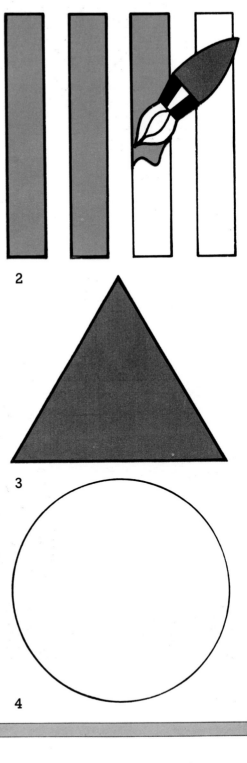

2

3

4

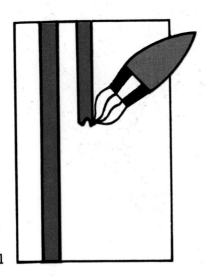

1

What you need
Stiff card
Pencil
Scissors
Paint or crayons
Glue
Gummed papers (optional)
Cotton wool balls
Powder paint

Parent's handy hint
The clown can be produced in any size and used as a hanging mobile by attaching a thread to the hat. While constructing the clown the child will assimilate shape, size and colour and gain a good knowledge of measurement.

5

6

7

Sets of Shapes

How to make it

1 Take a piece of strong card approximately 30 cm x 30 cm and by measuring half way along each edge and drawing across, divide into four squares.

2 Collect together sets of square items to decorate the squares.

3 Cover each square with strong glue and carefully stick on the items as neatly as possible.

4 Glue a loop of tape to the back to hang your sets on the wall.

5 A variation is shown using sets of circles including lentils, buttons and pasta.

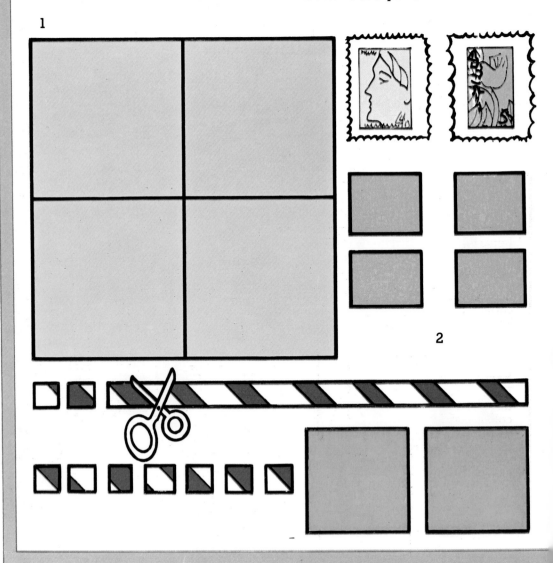

1

2

4

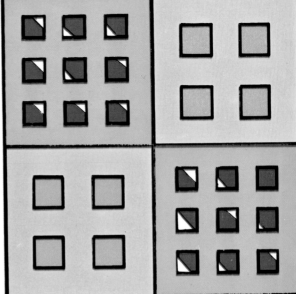

3

What you need
Strong card
Scissors
Ruler
Pencil
Items to decorate: material squares, stamps, coloured drinking straws cut into sections, gummed paper squares.
Strong glue
Tape

Parent's handy hint
Encourage the child to develop his own ideas of colour and shape in grouping items into sets for these projects. A three-dimensional effect can be created using painted matchboxes.

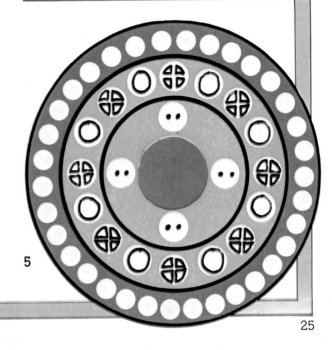

5

Halloween Party Pieces

Bat

How to make it

1   Decide on the size of bat you require and choose a piece of thin card or sugar paper twice as big. Fold it in half, draw on the bat shape and cut out from both halves, taking care *not* to cut the folded edge.
2   Open out the bat and paint or crayon it black.
3   Add the eyes from silver paper, sequins or other materials.

What you need

Thin card
Pencil
Scissors
Black paint or crayon
Silver paper, sequins (or
other materials) for eyes

Parent's handy hint

Stick the bat to a window,
suspend it from the ceil-
ing on elastic or glue it to
a pea stick to use as a
puppet. Single cat shapes
can also be suspended on
elastic to add atmosphere
to Halloween parties.

Party invitation

How to make it

1   Fold in half a piece of thin black
    card approximately 25 cm x 17
    cm. Draw on and cut out the cat
    shape from both halves taking
    care *not* to cut the folded edge.
2   Glue on red or green sequins
    for eyes.

Halloween Spider

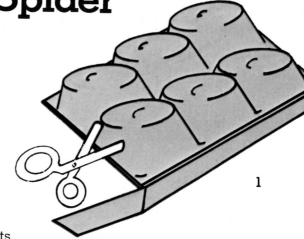

1

How to make it

1   Cut up a cardboard egg box
    and use the hollow the egg sits
    in for the spider's body.
2   Paint the body black.
3   Paint four pipe cleaners
    black and when dry cut in half.
4   Make four holes in each
    side of the body using a skewer.
5   Push each half pipe cleaner
    through a hole. Bend down
    approximately 1 cm inside and
    turn up the ends to shape the
    feet.
6   Glue eyes on to the body.
7   Pierce a hole through the top of
    the body and thread a piece of
    knotted elastic through.
    Suspend the spider from the
    ceiling.

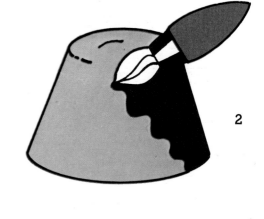

2

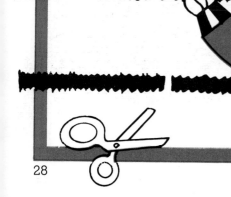

3

4

5

6

What you need
Cardboard egg box
Scissors
Black paint
4 pipe cleaners
Skewer
Buttons or sequins (or
other materials) for eyes
Glue
Narrow elastic
Parent's handy hint
Use a cardboard egg box
because it is easier to
paint. Show the child
how to use the skewer
safely.

7

Halloween Mask

1

How to make it

1   Take a square of thin card large enough to fit a child's face. Draw on the mask shape and cut it out.

2   Cut out the eyes, nose and mouth.

3   Make a hole at each side using a skewer.

4   Paint or crayon the mask orange and decorate around the eyes, nose and mouth in different colours.

5   Thread wool or narrow tape through the holes, knotting one end to secure. Tie in a bow behind the child's head.

2

3

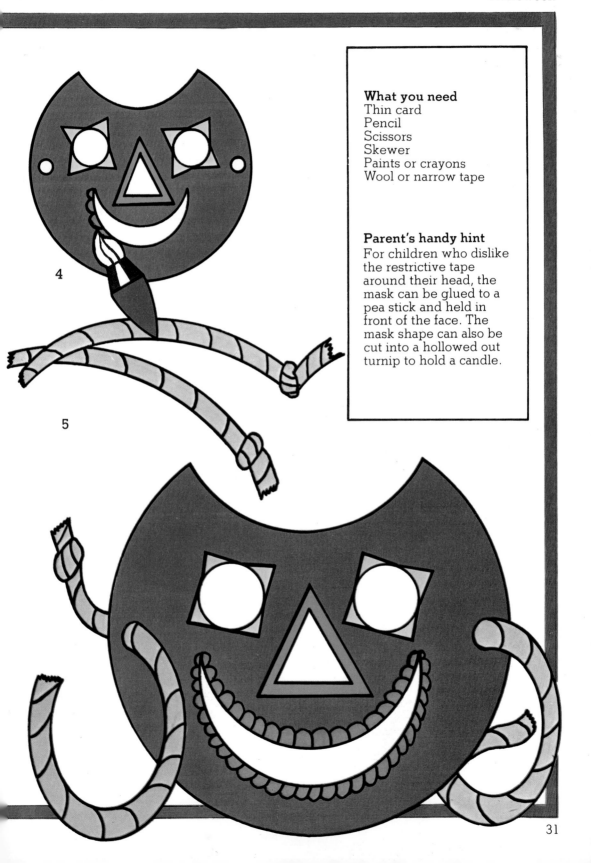

4

5

What you need
Thin card
Pencil
Scissors
Skewer
Paints or crayons
Wool or narrow tape

Parent's handy hint
For children who dislike
the restrictive tape
around their head, the
mask can be glued to a
pea stick and held in
front of the face. The
mask shape can also be
cut into a hollowed out
turnip to hold a candle.

Halloween Witch

How to make it

1 Cut a circle 30 cm across from black sugar paper and cut in half.

2 Take one semi-circle, place the straight edge at the top and fold down the top left hand corner to the centre bottom. Repeat with the other side so that the two sides overlap and glue together to make a cone.

3 Cut another circle 12 cm across from black sugar paper. Fold in half and make 2 cm cuts from the centre as shown.

4 Open out the circle and cut across the centre of the cuts to make a small hole. Glue the inside of the eight flaps and place the brim over the top of the cone, pressing the flaps down to stick. Cut a face shape from brightly coloured paper, draw on eyes, nose and mouth and glue under the brim.

5 Paint a drinking straw black.

6/7 Cut a strip of black crepe paper 12 cm x 7 cm and cut a fringe half way across along one edge. Glue the uncut side and roll on to the end of the straw to make a broomstick. Cut out a cat, decorate with glitter eyes and a collar to match the cloak, and glue to the broomstick. Make two holes through the witch using a skewer and push the broomstick through.

8 Take a strip of mauve crepe paper 8 cm x 20 cm and pleat glueing the top of each pleat down. Glue this to the witch's body underneath the hat.

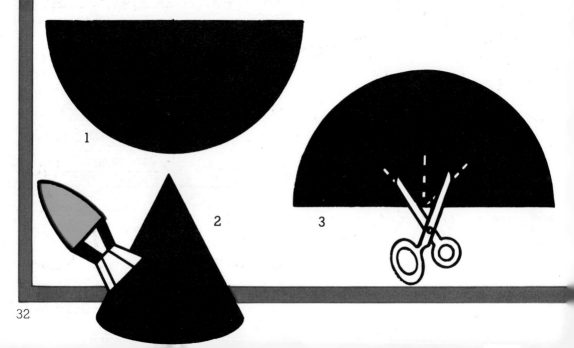

1

2

3

4

5

6

7

8

What you need
Black sugar paper
Scissors
Glue
Coloured paper
Felt-tipped pen
Drinking straw
Black paint
Black and mauve crepe
paper
Glitter
Skewer

Parent's handy hint
Show the child how to
prepare semi-circles from
the sugar paper. Unwaxed
drinking straws are easier
to paint than waxed.
Powder paint can be
thickened with made-up
wallpaper paste instead
of water.

Tube Santa

How to make it

1 Take a toilet roll tube and cut a piece of red crepe paper 15 cm longer than the tube. Lay the tube on the paper, fold it round and glue the long edges together to the top.

2/3 Push in and glue 2 cm at one end to secure and neaten the base. Pinch together the top and glue on a large cotton wool ball and a cotton wool strip to make a hat.

4 Draw a face on a piece of gummed paper and stick it on to Santa. Glue on a cotton wool beard and hair.

5 Cut out a strip of gummed paper for a belt and different coloured circles for buttons.

What you need
Toilet roll tube
Red crepe paper
Scissors
Glue
Cotton wool
Coloured gummed papers

Parent's handy hint
Have one or two spare
tubes handy for trial and
error. With crepe paper
always use a glue which
dries transparent and use
sparingly.

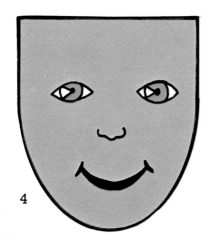

4

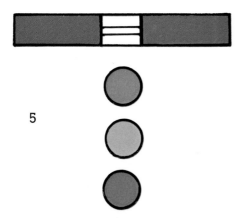

5

...ding Christmas Tree

How to make it

1   Take a toilet roll tube, paint and leave to dry.
2   Take a piece of green card approximately 20 cm x 15 cm and draw on a simple tree shape.
3   Cut out the tree, colour the trunk and decorate the container.

4/5 From a selection of coloured papers cut out various shapes to resemble decorations, including a star, and glue to the tree.
6   When dry, staple or glue the tree to the tube so that it stands up firmly.

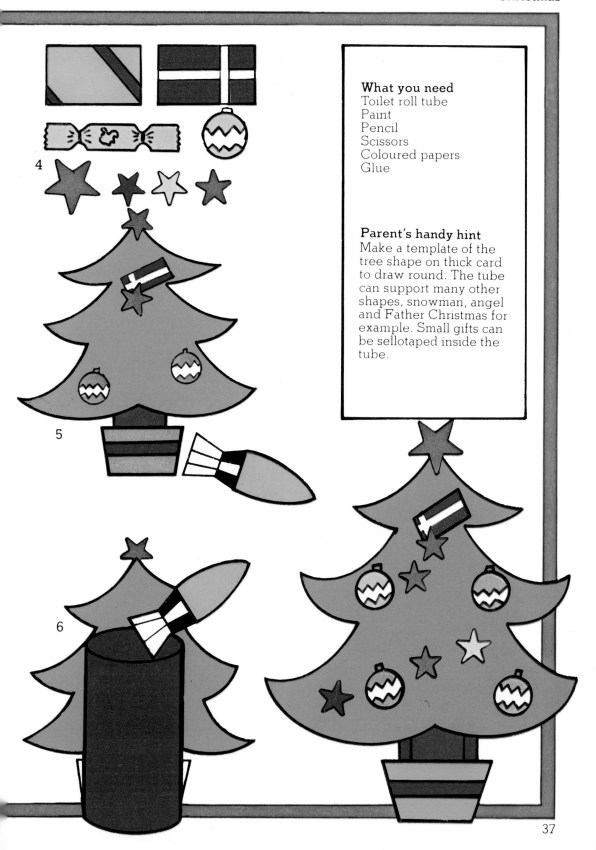

What you need
Toilet roll tube
Paint
Pencil
Scissors
Coloured papers
Glue

Parent's handy hint
Make a template of the
tree shape on thick card
to draw round. The tube
can support many other
shapes, snowman, angel
and Father Christmas for
example. Small gifts can
be sellotaped inside the
tube.

4

5

6

Bell Christmas Card

How to make it

1 Decide on the size of the bell you require and choose a piece of card twice as big.
2 Fold the card in half with the folded edge at the top.
3 Draw on the bell shape (see template on page 116).
4 Cut out the shape from both pieces of card taking care *not* to cut the top folded edge.
5 Decorate your bell with crayons or paints, or glue on silver or gold glitter, lampshade fringing or coloured paper.

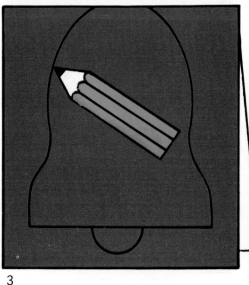

What you need
Card
Scissors
Pencil
Crayons or paints
Glitter (optional)
Lampshade fringing
(optional)
Coloured paper (optional)

Parent's handy hint
Make sure the top folded edge is not cut. Use the bells as Christmas tree decorations. Tiny bells can make parcel tags or name cards for table settings.

Do not cut here

4

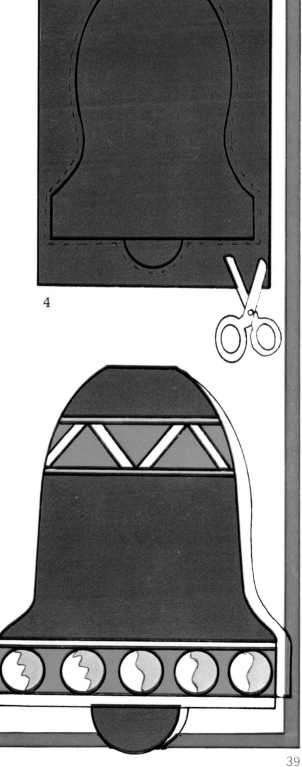

5

Christmas Angel

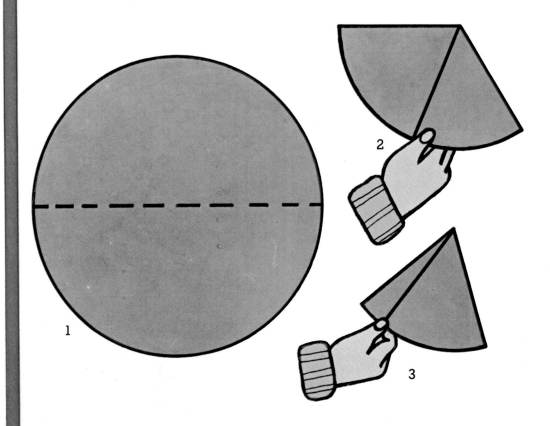

How to make it

1   Cut a circle 30 cm across from thin pink card and cut in half.

2   Take one semi-circle and with the straight edge at the top fold down the top right hand corner to the centre bottom.

3   Repeat with the other corner so that they overlap slightly and glue together to make a cone.

4   Cut out a pair of wings from pink card and two pairs from white crepe paper in the shape shown and put to one side.

5/6   Cut a strip of white crepe paper
/7   60 cm x 12 cm, pleat it tightly and glue it around the cone to make the angel's dress.

8   Glue one pair of white wings to the front of the pink pair and one to the back to give a translucent effect and staple the wings to the back of the angel. Draw in eyes, nose and mouth with felt-tipped pen and add a tinsel strip around the point of the cone.

4

5

What you need
Card
Scissors
Glue
White crepe paper
Stapler
Felt-tipped pen
Tinsel

Parent's handy hint
Demonstrate how to
make the cone and pleat
the crepe paper. The size
of the original circle will
determine the size of the
angel.

6

7

8

Three Kings and Mary

How to make them

1 Cut a circle of card 30 cm across and cut in half.
2 Cover one semi-circle with a brightly coloured material using a strong white glue and fold over to make a cone. Staple to secure.
3 Cut a small circle of pink card and draw on eyes, nose and mouth. Glue the face to the top of the cone.

4 Cut a smaller semi-circle of contrasting material and fold over 1 cm along the top edge. Glue this to the top of the face and the back of the head and fold in each side so that the cloak hangs freely.
5 Make crowns from decorated card and beards from cotton wool, fur or felt and glue in position.

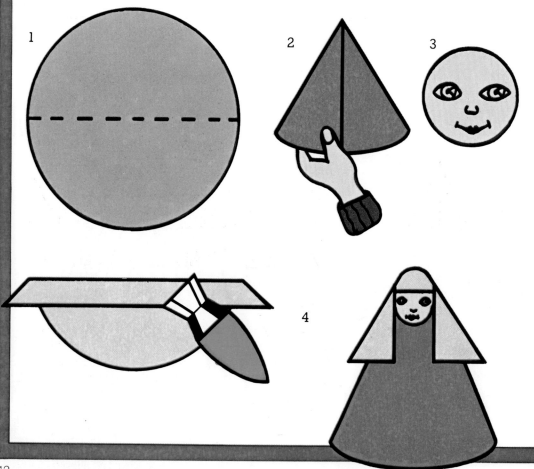

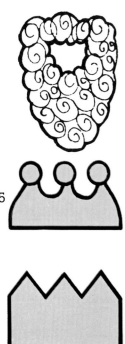

5

What you need
Card
Scissors
Brightly coloured material
Strong white glue
Stapler
Felt-tipped pen
Cotton wool, fur or felt

Parent's handy hint
These ideas are variations on the use of a cone (see pages 32 and 40). The models can be used to make a Nativity scene which can be displayed in a large painted card-board carton with the top and front removed. Use corrugated card to form a roof and floor. Shepherds can have hessian cloaks and the Christmas Bell idea (page 38) can be used to make sheep and other animals. Scatter wood shavings on the floor and use a matchbox to make a crib.

Christmas Party Hat

How to make it

1 Take a piece of card 10 cm wide and long enough to fit around the child's head plus a slight overlap. Glue or staple a piece of crepe paper 25 cm wide and the same length as the card to the bottom of the card as shown. This is the inside of the hat.

2 Bring the crepe paper over to cover the outside of the hat and bend the ends round to overlap. Glue and staple the two ends and gather the crepe paper together. Wrap sellotape round to hold it firmly.

3 Cut a piece of double sided foil 15 cm x 15 cm which tones with the crepe paper. Fold in half and cut narrow strips 5 cm long towards the fold.

4 Fold around the top of the hat and glue. Turn back the strips.

5 Cut another piece of foil 8 cm wide and the same length as the hat and cut a pattern as shown. Staple this around the hat to decorate.

6 Cut another piece of foil 40 cm x 16 cm and fold in half longways. Cut strips as before but this time across the fold to within 1 cm of the edge.

7 Take a pea stick approximately 15 cm long and sellotape one end of the folded and cut foil to the top (with the fold uppermost). Carefully wrap the foil around the stick to within 7 cm of the bottom and secure. Wrap foil round the bottom 7 cm and sellotape the stick to the hat.

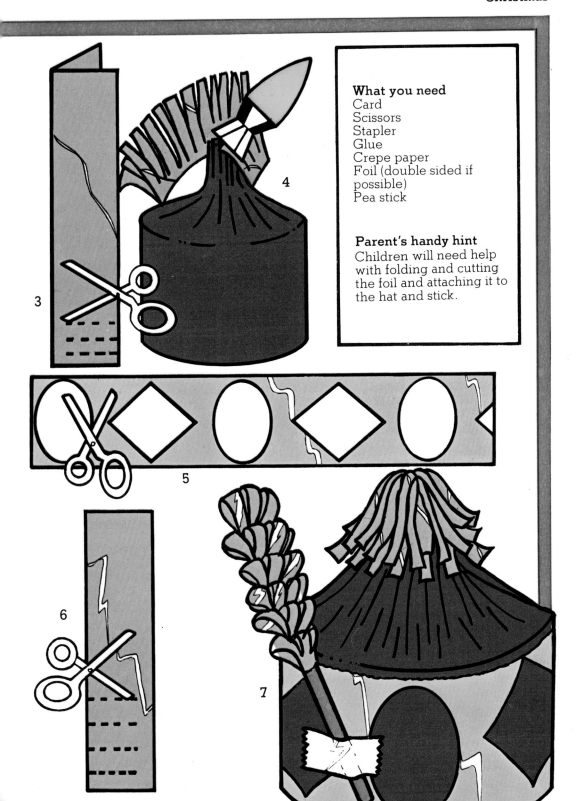

What you need
Card
Scissors
Stapler
Glue
Crepe paper
Foil (double sided if possible)
Pea stick

Parent's handy hint
Children will need help with folding and cutting the foil and attaching it to the hat and stick.

3

4

5

6

7

Country Church Calendar

How to make it

1 Take a piece of stiff blue card approximately 20 cm x 25 cm. This is the background.
2 Take a piece of black sugar paper approximately 15 cm x 18 cm and draw on the shape of a church.
3 Cut out the church.
4 Carefully cut out the window shapes and the door, leaving the left-hand edge to fold the door open.

5 Glue pieces of coloured foil paper to the back of the cut out windows.
6 Glue the church to the background card. Green felt can be added to the bottom to represent grass and white cotton wool to resemble snow.
7 Draw and cut out a clock and a star and glue them in position as shown. Use tape to attach the calendar and to make a picture hook.

1

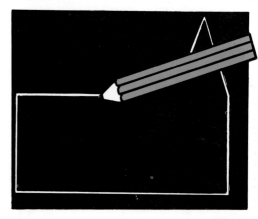

2

3

4

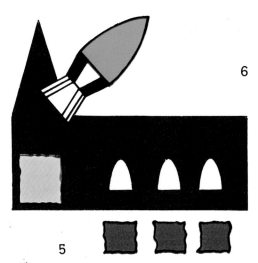

5

6

7

What you need
Stiff blue card
Black sugar paper
Pencil
Scissors
Coloured foil paper
Glue
White cotton wool
Green felt
Tape
Calendar

Parent's handy hint
Apply glue lightly to the
top of the steeple and
sprinkle with silver glitter
to give a frosty effect.
Take care to cut the door
just enough to open.

Calendar

Menorah

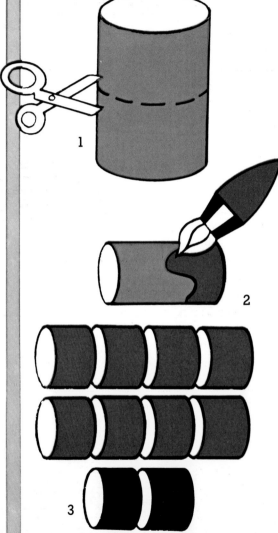

How to make it

1   Take five toilet roll tubes and cut four in half to make a total of nine candle holders.

2   Paint all the candle holders deep blue.

3   Cut one more toilet roll tube in half and paint it black to make two stands.

4   Cover a long narrow cereal box with gold or silver foil and glue on neatly.

5   Cut a band of stiff white paper and glue inside the top of each candle holder to represent a candle.

6   Cut flame shapes from yellow crepe paper and glue inside the top of each candle.

7   Glue all the candle holders firmly to the top of the cereal box with the tall one in front of the centre. Glue the two stands underneath the box spacing well apart.

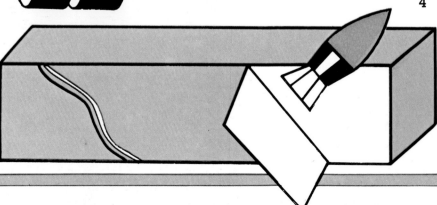

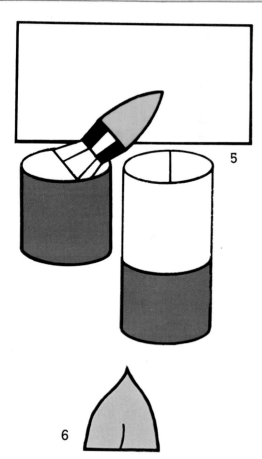

5

6

What you need
6 toilet roll tubes
Scissors
Black and blue paint
Cereal box
Gold or silver foil
Glue
Stiff white paper
Yellow crepe paper

Parent's handy hint
A useful project to stimu-
late discussion about the
Jewish festival Chanukah.
See also Chanukah Latkes
on page 112.

7

ntine Card

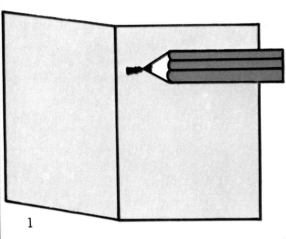

1

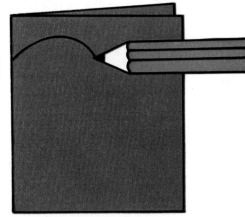

2

3

How to make it

1   Take a piece of card approxi-
    mately 17 cm x 21 cm, fold in
    half and write a message inside.

2   Now fold a piece of coloured
    gummed paper in half. Draw
    half a heart shape up to the left-
    hand folded edge.

3   From the folded edge cut out
    the heart shape from both
    pieces of paper leaving the
    folded edge uncut.

4   Unfold the heart. You now have
    a symmetrical heart shape. Glue
    the heart to the front of the
    card.

5   Tear brightly coloured tissue
    paper in small pieces and
    crumple into balls.

6   Glue the balls around the edge
    of the heart shape and write 'To
    my Valentine' on the front.

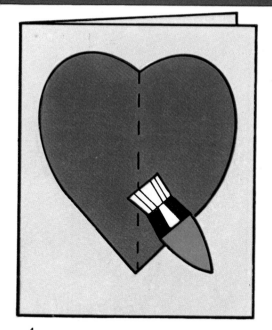

4

What you need
Card
Pencil and felt-tipped pen
Scissors
Coloured gummed paper
Glue
Coloured tissue paper

Parent's handy hint
Practice making the heart
and explain the principle
of a symmetrical shape.
Alternative materials for
the heart could be foil or
velvet trimmed with
pinking shears.

5/6

To
My
Valentine

Valentine Basket

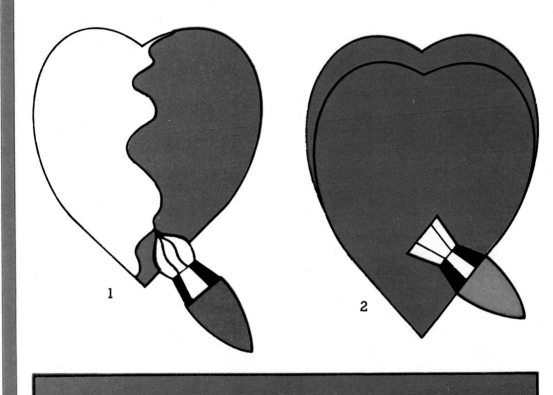

1

2

3

How to make it

1   Take two pieces of stiff card approximately 25 cm x 20 cm and draw and cut out two matching heart shapes. Paint or felt-tip them a delicate colour.

2   Glue the sides of the hearts together leaving the top open. When dry gently push the sides in to open the basket.

3/4 Cut a strip of felt 1 cm x 45 cm in the same colour, or pleasantly contrasting, and glue into the top of the basket to make a handle.

4   Cut out two smaller matching hearts from coloured gummed paper (see Valentine Card on page 50 for the method) and glue one to the front and one to the back of the basket.

5   Glue lace to the top of the basket and sequins around the edge. The word 'Valentine' can be written on the smaller front heart.

4

What you need
Stiff card
Pencil
Paint or felt-tipped pen
Glue
Felt
Coloured gummed paper
Lace
Sequins

Parent's handy hint
Can hold a small packet
of sweets, a fancy hand-
kerchief, a bottle of
perfume or a lavender
sachet. Can be adapted
to an Easter Basket to
hold eggs.

5

Mother's Day House

How to make it

1 Take a piece of card approximately 21 cm x 30 cm and draw and cut out the house outline as shown.

2 Decorate the roof with coloured adhesive tape.

3/4 Cut out suitable pictures of mothers from old catalogues or magazines and glue these to the front of the house.

5 Take another piece of card 12 cm x 10 cm to make the door and cover with wallpaper.

6 Fold over 1 cm along the long edge and glue this flap to the front of the house. Add a paper fastener for a door knob.

7 Find a small photograph of your mother and glue it behind the door so that it is hidden when the door is closed.

8 Add this message to the front of the card:
'Mothers come in all shapes and sizes but only one...' and finish it off above the photograph of Mother with '...fits this house just right'.

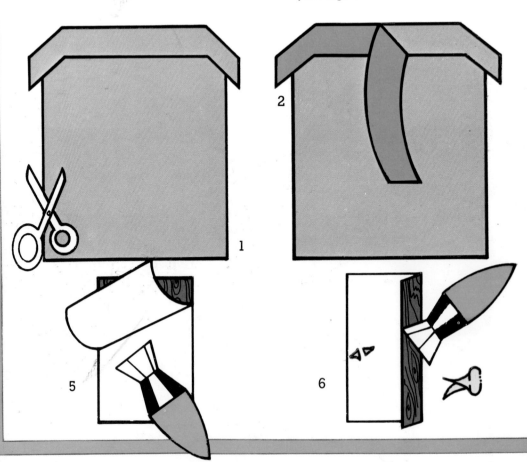

3

What you need
Card
Pencil
Scissors
Coloured adhesive tape
Old catalogues or
magazines
Glue
Wallpaper
Paper fastener
Photograph of Mother

Parent's handy hint
Save all your old maga-
zines and catalogues as a
source of pictures for
crafty ideas. This card
can be modified to suit
Father.

4

8

7

Mother
comes
in all
shapes
and
sizes
but only
one....

er's Day Card

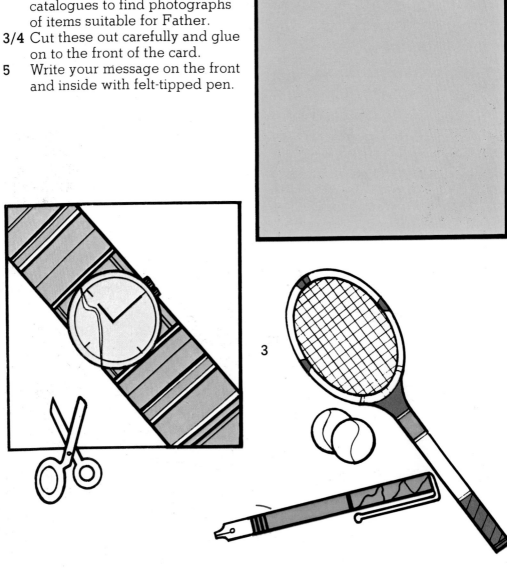

How to make it

1. Take a piece of card approximately 21 cm x 17 cm (shirt box card is suitable) and fold it in half.
2. Look through old mail order catalogues to find photographs of items suitable for Father.
3/4. Cut these out carefully and glue on to the front of the card.
5. Write your message on the front and inside with felt-tipped pen.

2

What you need

Card
Scissors
Mail order catalogues
Glue
Felt-tipped pen

Parent's handy hint

An easy-to-make card which can be adapted for Mother's Day, birthdays and other occasions by the choice of cut out items.

4

5

Happy Father's Day

essed Flower Bookmark

1

How to make it
1   Have ready a selection of dried and pressed flowers and leaves.
2   Take a piece of thick card approximately 23 cm x 4 cm.
3   Carefully cut a fringe 4 cm into the length of the card.
4   Using a strong transparent glue, gently place the flowers in position.
5   Allow the glue to dry for several hours and then cover the bookmark with transparent covering film. An alternative version for Father can be made using stamps.

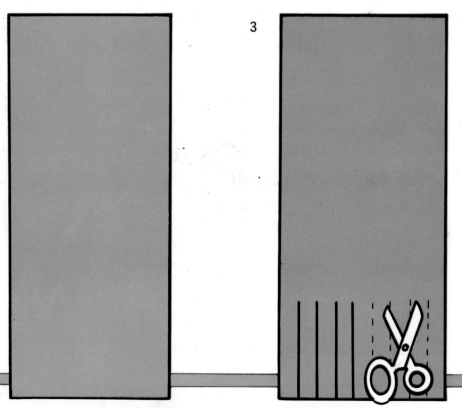

2

3

4

What you need

Dried and pressed flowers
and leaves
Thick card
Pencil
Scissors
Strong glue
Transparent covering film

Parent's handy hint

The flowers can be bought
but try drying your own.
Place them between blot-
ting paper and leave
under a heavy weight for
two weeks.

5

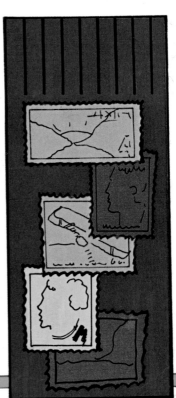

1

Collage on Polystyrene

How to make it

1 Take a large polystyrene tile.

2 Draw sections on it with a felt-tipped pen. Some sections can be covered with material to make a background colour onto which beads or sequins can be pasted.

3 Gather together as many different items as possible to decorate your tile.

4 Cover one section with strong wallpaper paste and carefully stick on the items for that section.

5 Start a new section only when the previous one is completed. Continue until the tile is covered.

6 Glue a loop of tape to the top to

2

3

4

hang your collage as a wall picture.

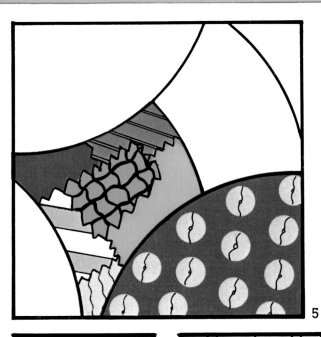

5

What you need
Large polystyrene ceiling tile
Felt-tipped pen
Items to decorate:
material, sequins, beads, stamps, bus tickets, dried herbs, lentils, tissue paper
Strong wallpaper paste
Glue
Tape

Parent's handy hint
Look through the kitchen cupboard for natural items for this project. Add a calendar to make a Christmas gift.

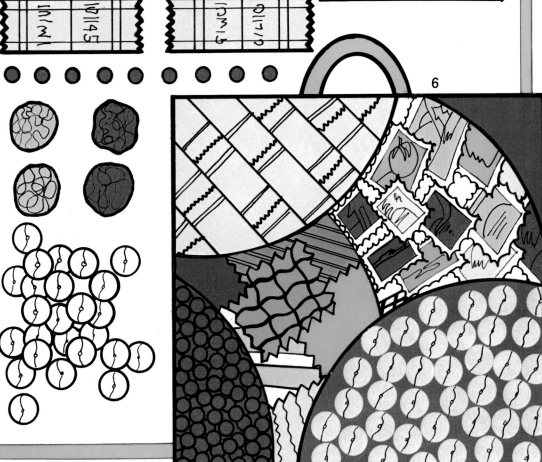

6

Yoghurt Carton Gift Holder

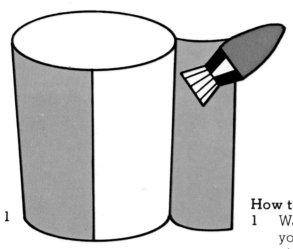

1

2

How to make it

1   Wash and thoroughly dry a yoghurt carton and cover with pink gummed paper.

2   Cut narrow strips of crepe paper for hair and glue the top of each strip inside the carton. Glue a narrow band of paper round the inside of the carton to tidy and secure the hair.

3   Cut a circle of stiff green card slightly larger than the carton and glue on crumpled balls of brightly coloured tissue paper.

4   Cut out eyes, nose and mouth from felt or gummed paper and stick on. Add a frill of lace to the hat and neck.

What you need
Yoghurt carton
Pink gummed paper
Scissors
Crepe paper
Glue
Stiff green card
Tissue paper
Felt or gummed papers
Strip of lace

Parent's handy hint
The hat is a lid and the
holder can contain a
packet of sweets for a
birthday gift, an Easter
egg wrapped in silver foil
or cotton wool balls for a
Mother's Day gift.

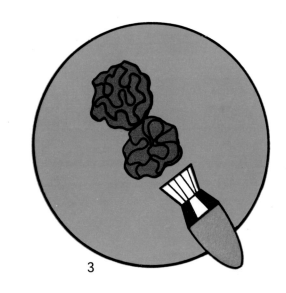

3

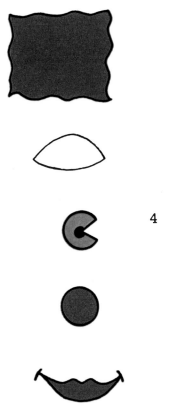

4

liceman Pencil Holder

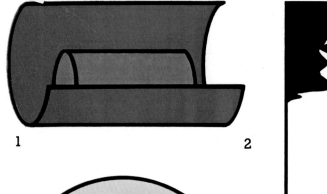

1

2

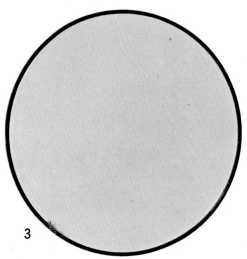

3

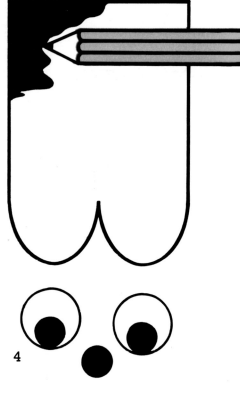

4

How to make it

1 Take a toilet roll tube and cover with blue gummed paper to make the body.

2 Cut out the feet from card and cover with black gummed paper or crayon black.

3/4 Cut out a circle 10 cm across from pink card and add eyes, nose and mouth from gummed paper shapes, or use a felt-tipped pen.

5 Cut out a helmet shape from card and cover with blue gummed paper. Add a badge from silver paper.

6/7 Glue on strands of wool or wood shavings to resemble hair and a moustache.

8 Glue the head and the feet firmly to the body and add silver paper buttons to the body. Keep your pencils in the tube.

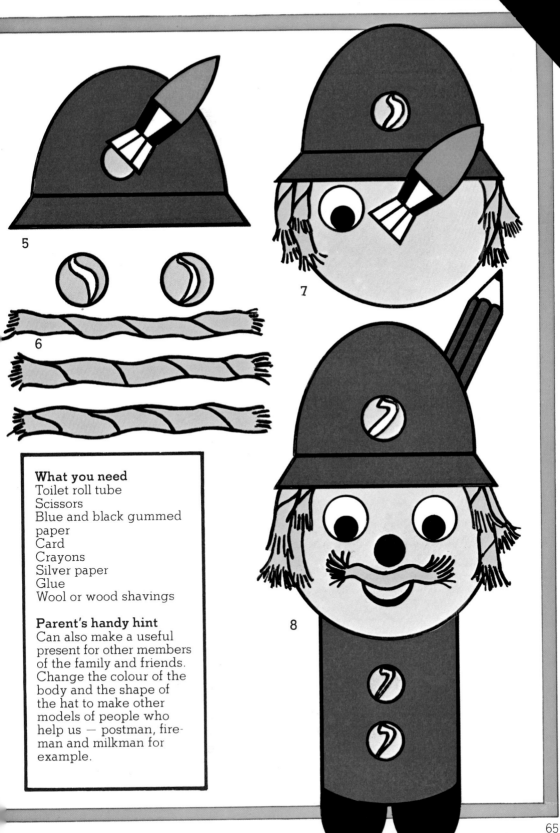

5

6

7

What you need
Toilet roll tube
Scissors
Blue and black gummed
paper
Card
Crayons
Silver paper
Glue
Wool or wood shavings

Parent's handy hint
Can also make a useful
present for other members
of the family and friends.
Change the colour of the
body and the shape of
the hat to make other
models of people who
help us — postman, fire-
man and milkman for
example.

8

...ndy Jotter

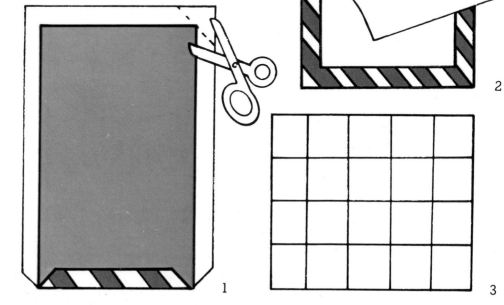

1

2

3

How to make it

1 Take a piece of stiff card approximately 20 cm x 12 cm and cover with wallpaper, cutting and glueing as shown.

2 Cut a piece of paper slightly smaller than the card and glue to the back.

3 Cut twenty pieces of white paper approximately 11 cm square from one large piece as shown or from scraps.

4 Take the first piece of paper and glue the top edge firmly to the front of the jotter leaving about 4 cm at the bottom.

5 Glue each individual sheet in this way to the one below and punch a hole through the centre top of the jotter.

6 Take a tiny pencil and 2 cm of Velcro. Glue half to the pencil and half to the jotter and attach the pencil. Hang the jotter from a piece of ribbon, tape or cord threaded through the hole.

4

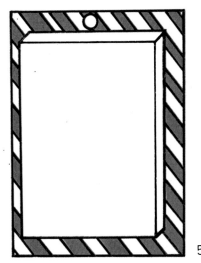

5

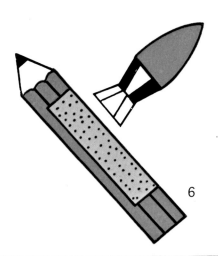

6

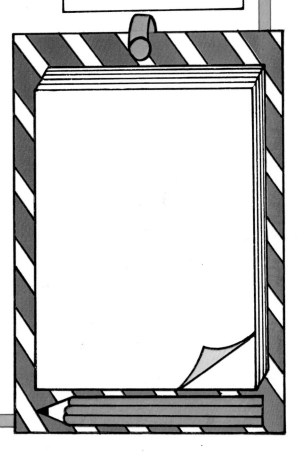

What you need
Stiff card
Scissors
Wallpaper
Glue
Paper
Skewer
Small pencil
Piece of Velcro
Piece of ribbon, tape or cord

Parent's handy hint
Encourage your child to carry out the measuring and cutting involved in this project which will help develop skills of precision.

Egg-shaped Card

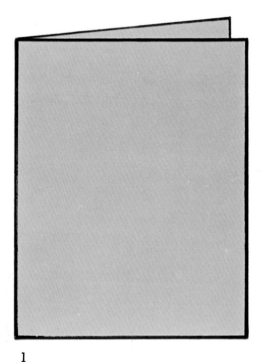

1

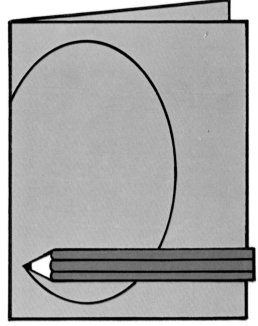

2

How to make it

1   Take a piece of card approximately 20 cm x 25 cm and fold it in half.
2   Draw a large egg shape on the front.
3   Cut out the shape from both pieces of card taking care *not* to cut folded left edge. You should now have two eggs joined together at the left-hand side.
4   Cut out a large number of very small circles from coloured tissue paper.

5   Starting from the bottom of the front egg, glue each circle onto the card, making sure that only the top is attached. In this way the circles will overlap. Leave a gap about 2 cm wide across the middle.
6   Glue a row of brightly coloured tissue paper balls across the middle to look like a ribbon. Write an appropriate greeting inside the egg.

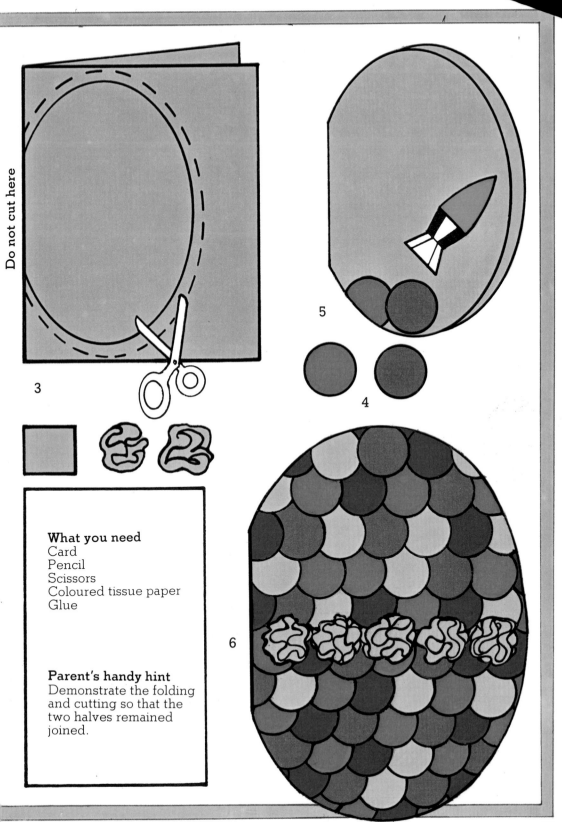

Do not cut here

3

5

4

6

What you need
Card
Pencil
Scissors
Coloured tissue paper
Glue

Parent's handy hint
Demonstrate the folding
and cutting so that the
two halves remained
joined.

69

Fluffy Easter Card

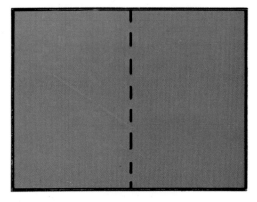

1

Do not cut here

2

3

How to make it

1   Take a piece of card approximately 20 cm x 25 cm and fold it in half.
2   Draw an Easter chick on the front.
3   Cut out the shape from both pieces of card taking care *not* to cut the folded left edge.
4   Open out the card and colour a border of small Easter eggs all the way round the inside.
5/6 Cut out pieces of felt and glue on for the eyes and beak. Roll tiny balls of yellow cotton wool and glue to the front of the chick. (The Easter bunny alternative could have a white cotton wool tail and whiskers from glued paper.) Write a greeting inside the card.

4

5

6

What you need
Card
Pencil
Scissors
Cotton wool balls
(preferably yellow)
Brightly coloured felt

Parent's handy hint
Any animal shape can be
used. Younger children
will need help with the
cutting out.

Easter Bonnet

How to make it

1 Rub the outside of the margarine tub with a scouring pad to remove the wax surface.

2 Tear a sheet of coloured tissue paper into small pieces and screw into balls.

3 Cut strips of the same width but varying length from tissue paper using several different colours.

4 Cut two strips of crepe paper long enough to reach from the top of the bonnet to underneath the chin in a bow.

5/6 Glue all the paper strips to the centre of the bonnet starting with one long crepe paper strip on each side, finishing off by covering the entire top half with the tissue paper balls.

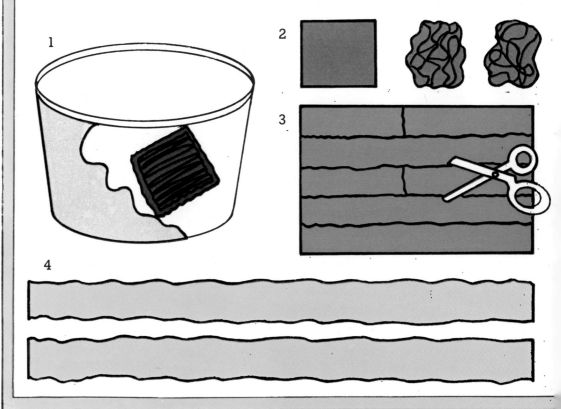

5

6

What you need
Margarine tub
Scouring pad
Coloured tissue paper
Scissors
Crepe paper
Glue

Parent's handy hint
The scouring pad removes
the wax surface so that
the glue adheres more
easily. The Easter Bonnet
can be used as a Christmas
party hat.

Easter Chicks

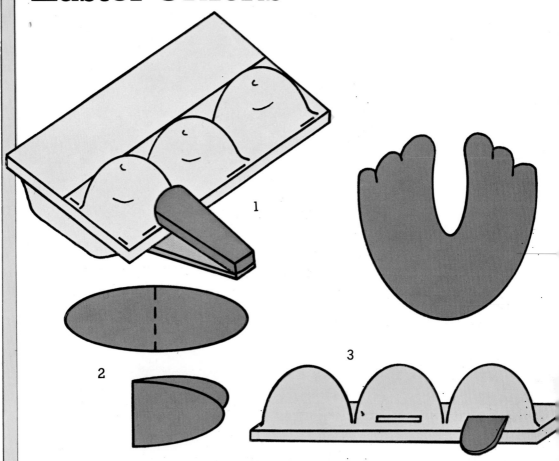

How to make it

1   Take two polystyrene egg boxes of different colours. Carefully remove the fastening flap (used later) and cut the lid in half longways. Staple the front three egg sections securely to the base.

2   Cut out beaks and feet from pieces of brightly coloured card using the patterns shown here as a guide. Fold the beak in half.

3   Make a small slit in the front of each egg section and insert each beak.

4   Draw in eyes using a felt-tipped pen and glue the feet into place using a plastic based glue.

5   Cut out the small raised pieces from the fastening flap and glue on to the chick's heads. Pierce a hole in the back of each chick's head with a darning needle and insert a brightly coloured feather for a tail.

What you need
2 polystyrene egg boxes
in different colours
Scissors
Stapler
Coloured card
Felt-tipped pen
Plastic based glue
Darning needle
Coloured feathers

Parent's handy hint
Use egg boxes of different
colours so that the hats
will contrast with the
chicks. Use a feather
duster to obtain coloured
feathers.

4

5

Stained Glass Window

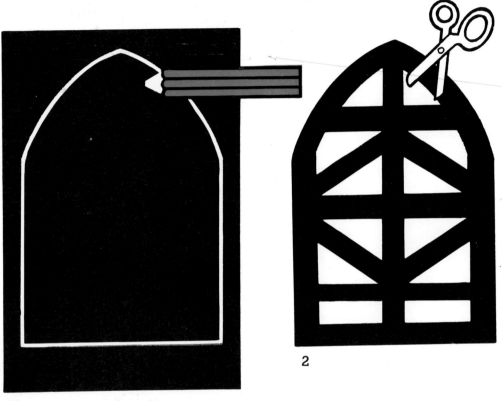

1

2

How to make it

1   Choose a piece of black or coloured sugar paper the size you require for your window Draw on the arch shape and cut it out.

2   Using the above pattern as a guide draw and then cut out the sections of the windows.

3   Cut out pieces of coloured tissue paper slightly larger than the window sections.

4   Lightly glue the back of the surrounding area of each section and gently position the tissue paper over it. Continue until each section is covered.

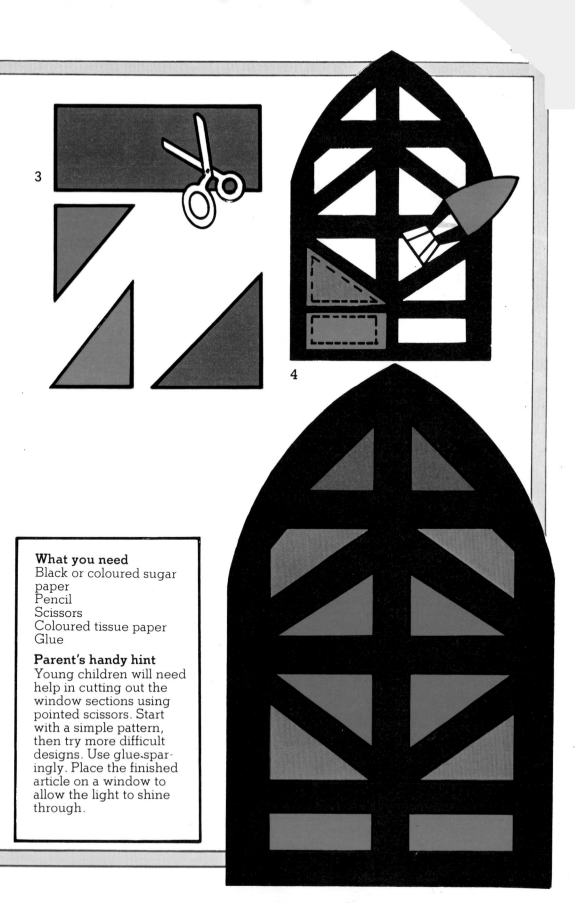

3

4

What you need
Black or coloured sugar paper
Pencil
Scissors
Coloured tissue paper
Glue

Parent's handy hint
Young children will need help in cutting out the window sections using pointed scissors. Start with a simple pattern, then try more difficult designs. Use glue sparingly. Place the finished article on a window to allow the light to shine through.

aster Basket

How to make it

1 Take a piece of stiff card approximately 11 cm x 25 cm and cut off a strip 2 cm wide to use for a handle.

2 Fold the large piece of card round and secure the edges with staples.

3 Cut a circle from another piece of card approximately 11 cm across and make cuts 1.5 cm deep all round the edge. Glue the bottom 2 cm of the 'tube' and stick the base to it, pressing the cut strips firmly on to the glued surface.

4 Cut a piece of crepe paper large enough to cover the outside of the basket and glue securely inside.

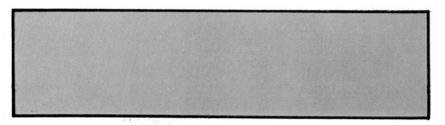

1

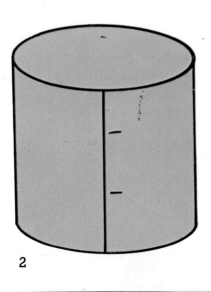

2

3

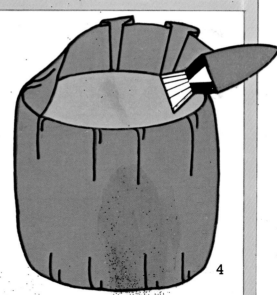

5 Cut two strips of crepe paper in different colours and wind around the strip of card for the handle. Glue and staple the handle to the basket.

6 Crumple small pieces of coloured tissue paper into balls and glue them all over the basket.

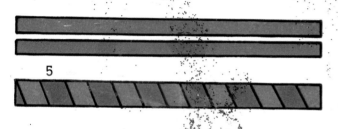

5

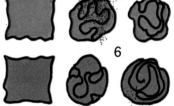

6

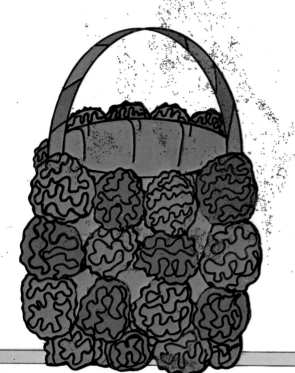

What you need
Stiff card
Scissors
Stapler
Glue
Coloured crepe paper
Coloured tissue papers

Parent's handy hint
A useful Easter gift holder especially for home made sweets. If an egg is to be placed inside, judge the length of card required before you cut it.

Standing Flower Place Card

How to make it

1/2 Choose a colourful flower from an old birthday card and cut it out carefully.

3 Cut a piece of coloured card approximately 8 cm x 6 cm to use as the base.

4 Cut another strip approximately 6 cm x 2 cm to make the holding strip. Fold over 2 cm.

5 Glue the fold to the base and the cut out flower to the upright.

6 Write the name of each guest on the front of your place card.

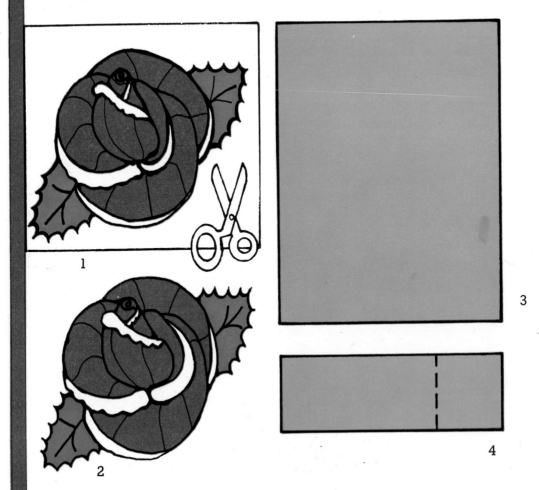

1

2

3

4

What you need
Old birthday cards
Scissors
Coloured card
Glue
Pencil

Parent's handy hint
A different flower for
each place card results in
an attractive table display.

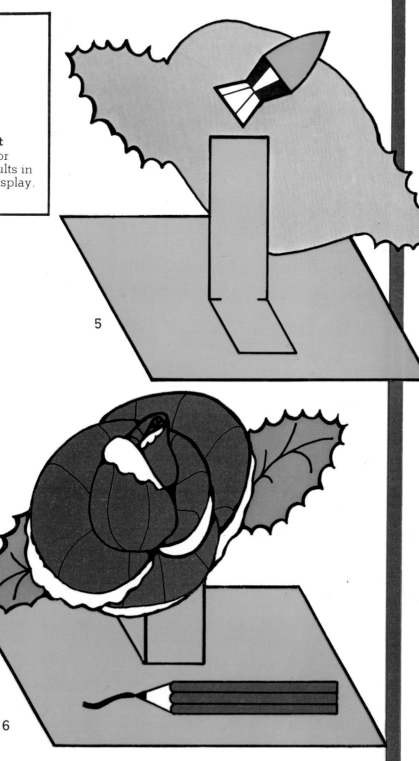

5

6

Toothbrush Holder

How to make it

1   Wash and thoroughly dry a yoghurt carton.
2   Cut out a selection of small pieces of brightly coloured materials.
3   Make a fancy edge to each piece with pinking shears.
4   Stick the material pieces on to the outside of the carton using strong white glue so that they overlap to make an interesting pattern.

1

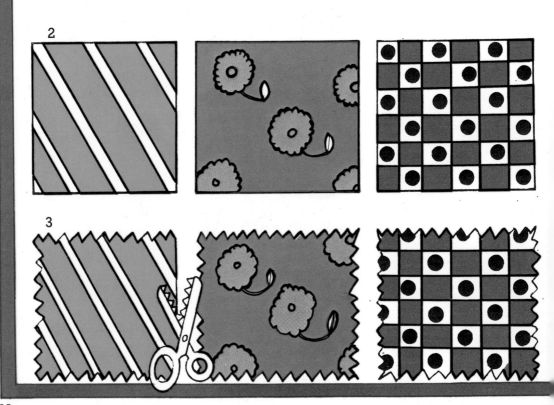

2

3

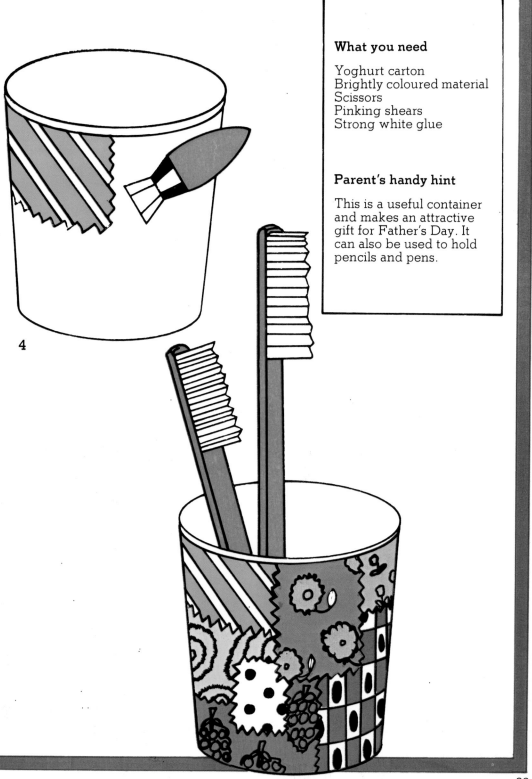

What you need

Yoghurt carton
Brightly coloured material
Scissors
Pinking shears
Strong white glue

Parent's handy hint

This is a useful container and makes an attractive gift for Father's Day. It can also be used to hold pencils and pens.

4

Psychedelic Wallpaper

1

How to make it

1 Take a square of 'anaglypta' wallpaper with a raised design. Any size will do.
2 Trim all around the edges with pinking shears.
3 Start colouring a section of the raised pattern with a felt-tipped pen.
4/5 Using different colours for different parts of the pattern complete your square.

2

3

4

What you need

Wallpaper with a raised
pattern ('anaglypta')
Scissors
Pinking shears
Felt-tipped pen

Parent's handy hint

An excellent way of using
up old wallpaper to make
an attractive and unusual
wall decoration or place
mat. Can also be pasted
on to an old cupboard or
door to give it a new look.
Use wallpaper paste
suitable for heavy papers.

5

Eskimo Pen Holder

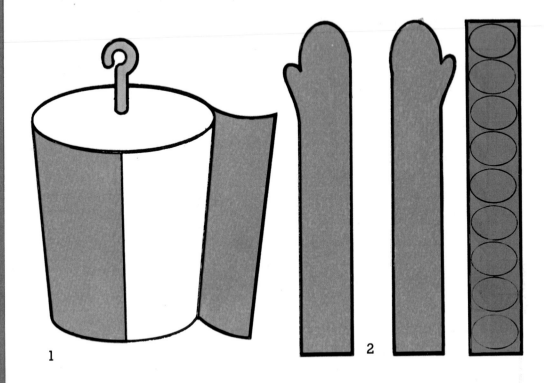

1

2

How to make it

1   Wash and thoroughly dry a yoghurt carton, and turn it upside down. With a skewer make a hole large enough to hold a pen through the bottom. Now cover the carton with brightly coloured gummed paper.

2   Cut out arm shapes as shown from the same paper and a belt from paper of a contrasting colour. Glue on arms and belt.

3/4   Take a pink tissue and wrap it around a ball of cotton wool to make a head and glue to secure. Glue this firmly to the bottom of the carton towards the front and draw on eyes, nose and mouth with felt-tipped pen.

5/6   Cut a piece of felt into an oval shape and add cotton wool as shown. Glue this to the back of the head to look like a fur hat. Glue a cotton wool 'fur' trim to the base and place a pen or pencil in the hole.

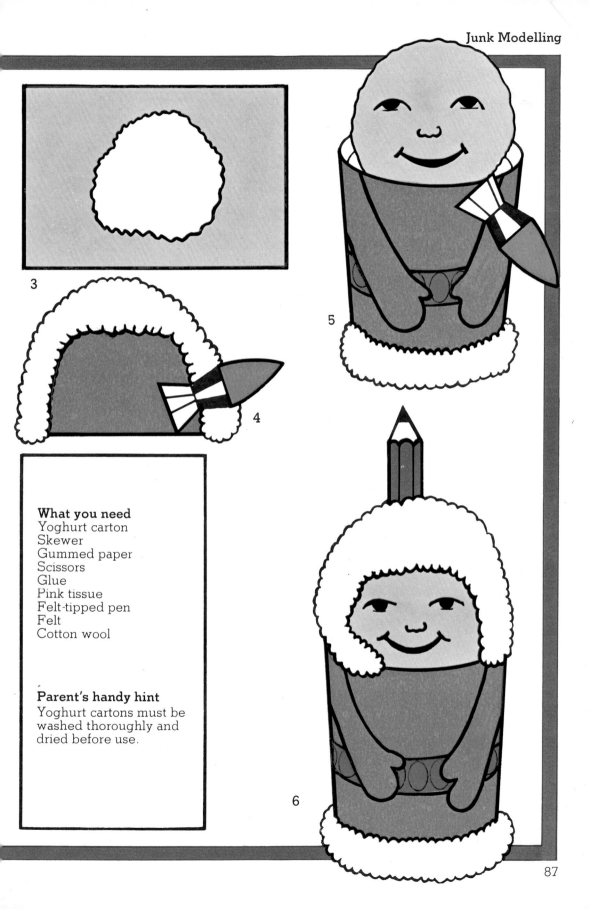

3

4

5

6

What you need
Yoghurt carton
Skewer
Gummed paper
Scissors
Glue
Pink tissue
Felt-tipped pen
Felt
Cotton wool

Parent's handy hint
Yoghurt cartons must be
washed thoroughly and
dried before use.

Egg Box Butterfly

How to make it

1   Take a cardboard egg box and cut off the lid.
2   Cut the base in half longways to give three egg sections and paint these a bright colour.
3   Cut out a pair of wings from thin card in the shape shown and paint or crayon them in a pattern of your choice.
4   Make a slit on either side of the centre egg section and gently push the narrow end of the wings through. Bend down the ends inside and secure with sellotape.

5   Make two holes in the first egg section with a skewer. Take a pipe cleaner and cut in half. Push half through one hole and out through the other to make antennae. Finish off by drawing on a face with felt-tipped pen.

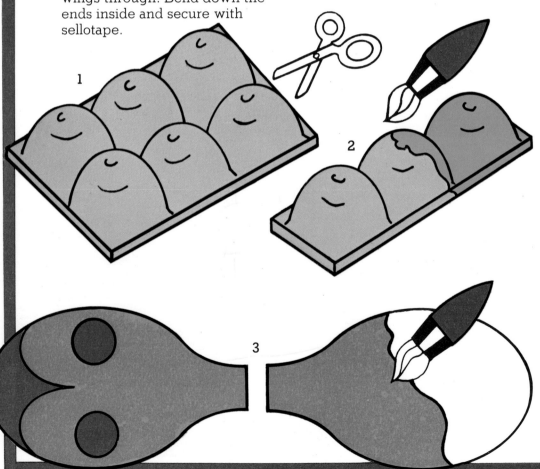

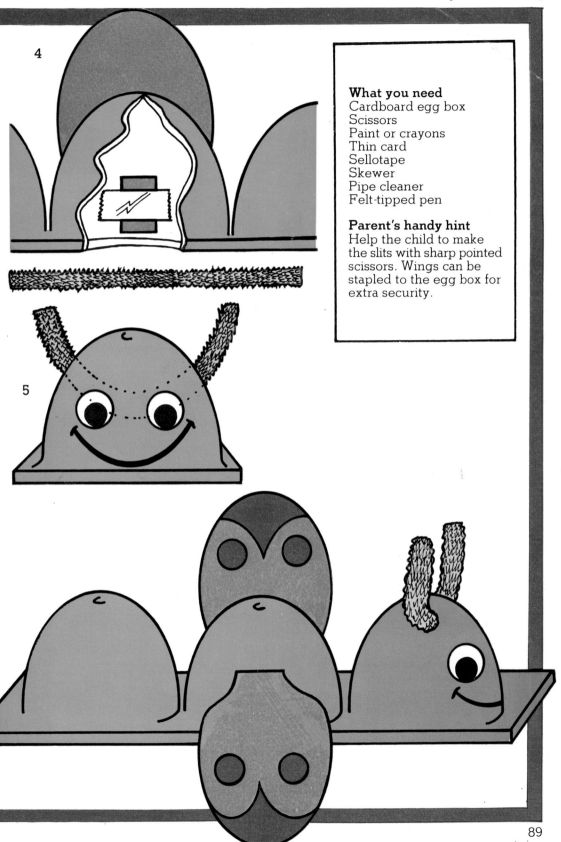

4

What you need
Cardboard egg box
Scissors
Paint or crayons
Thin card
Sellotape
Skewer
Pipe cleaner
Felt-tipped pen

Parent's handy hint
Help the child to make
the slits with sharp pointed
scissors. Wings can be
stapled to the egg box for
extra security.

5

Window Box

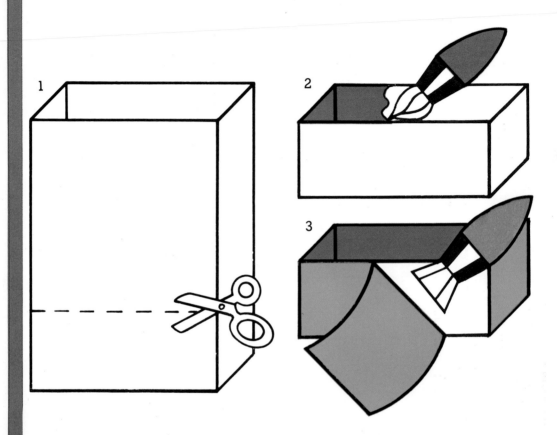

How to make it

1 Take a cereal box and cut across to leave a base 8 cm high.
2 Paint the inside brown to resemble soil.
3 Cover the outside with coloured gummed paper or wallpaper.
4 Cut out this flower shape several times from brightly coloured tissue papers.
5 Cut out this leaf shape several times from green tissue paper.
6 Take a piece of green tissue paper 14 cm x 9 cm and roll up and glue the long edge to make a stalk. Glue the flowers around the stalk and add the leaves.
7 Glue the completed flowers to a strip of card 2 cm deep and 3 cm longer than the box. Fold over 1.5 cm at each end and glue the folded ends firmly to the inside of the box so that the stalks rest on the bottom.

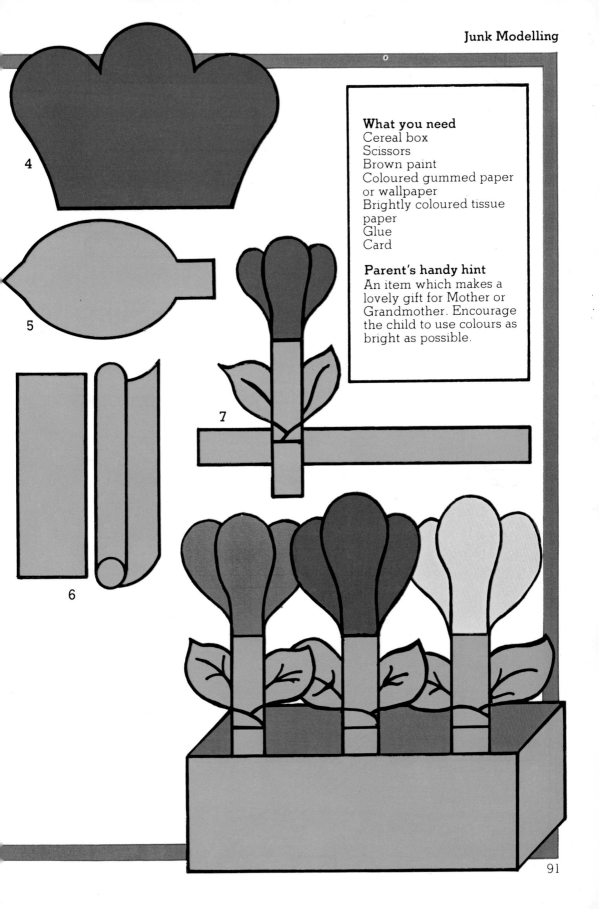

4

5

6

7

What you need
Cereal box
Scissors
Brown paint
Coloured gummed paper
or wallpaper
Brightly coloured tissue
paper
Glue
Card

Parent's handy hint
An item which makes a
lovely gift for Mother or
Grandmother. Encourage
the child to use colours as
bright as possible.

Paper Bag Puppet

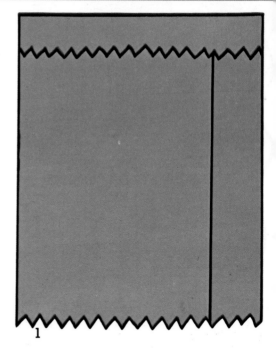

How to make it

1   Take a strong brown paper bag.
2   Cut out two large slits for eyes
    and draw on a nose and mouth
    with a felt-tipped pen.
3   Twist the top corners to make
    ears and glue on strands of
    yellow wool for hair.
4   Cut out thin strips of black
    paper and glue on to make
    whiskers.
5   Take a long cardboard tube,
    paint and leave to dry.
6   Fill the bag with balls of
    crumpled newspaper and secure
    it to the tube with an elastic
    band.

What you need
Strong brown paper bag
Scissors
Felt-tipped pen
Yellow wool
Black paper
Glue
Long cardboard tube
(silver foil tube)
Paint
Newspaper
Elastic band

Parent's handy hint
Many characters can be
made in this way to make
a puppet show.

Pasta Shell Bracelet

How to make it

1 Cut an empty washing-up liquid bottle into circles using sharp scissors.
2 Wash and dry the rings well.
3 Put a quantity of thick white glue into a clean margarine carton and add enough dry powder paint to give a rich colour.
4 Paint each bracelet with the glue and immediately place the pasta shells in position all the way round. Cover the remaining glue until needed for **5**. Allow the bracelet to set hard.
5 Paint the shells with the same glue mixture.

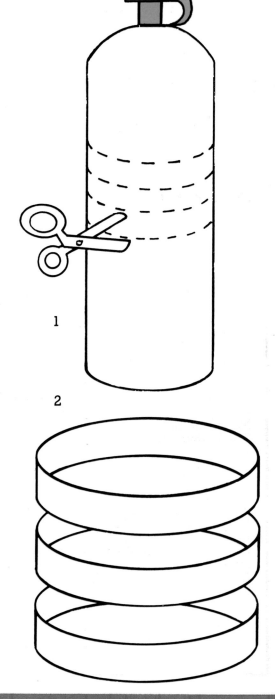

1

2

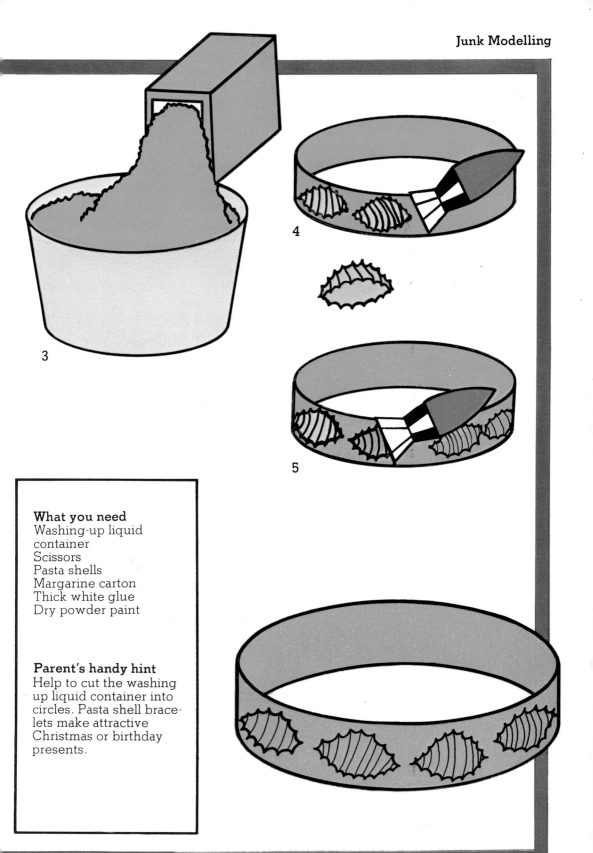

3

4

5

What you need
Washing-up liquid
container
Scissors
Pasta shells
Margarine carton
Thick white glue
Dry powder paint

Parent's handy hint
Help to cut the washing
up liquid container into
circles. Pasta shell brace-
lets make attractive
Christmas or birthday
presents.

Exotic Birds Mobile

How to make it

1 Take a piece of card approximately 50 cm x 45 cm, draw on the tree shape and cut it out.
2 Crayon or paint both sides to look like a tree.
3 Cut out the basic shapes of four birds from coloured card.
4/5 Pleat four small pieces of crepe paper and make a slit with sharp pointed scissors through the centre of each bird's body.
6 Insert the pleated paper wings and adjust to different angles.

7 Cut narrow strips of different coloured tissue paper and glue or staple to each bird's tail.
8 Using a darning needle make a small hole in the centre top of each bird's body, and at the end of each branch, and suspend the birds with cotton. Suspend the whole mobile from the ceiling or a light fitting.

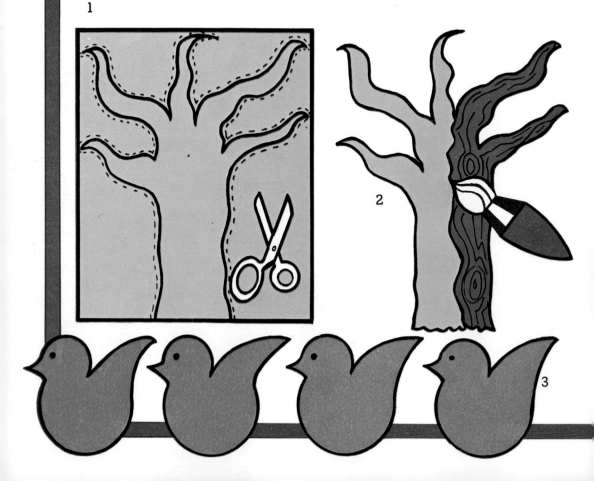

What you need
Card
Pencil
Scissors
Crayons or paints
Crepe paper
Coloured tissue paper
Glue
Darning needle
Cotton

Parent's handy hint
Supervise making holes with the darning needle in the right position for the birds to hang correctly. Help to suspend the mobile from the ceiling or light fitting.

4

5

6

7

8

Moving Tanker

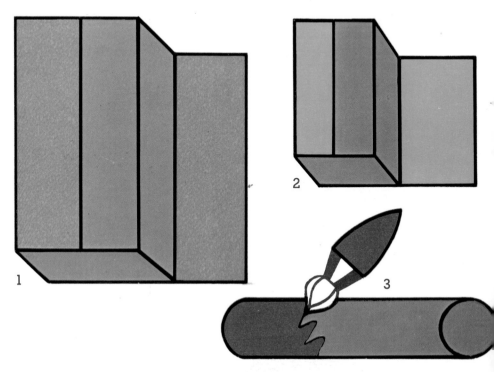

How to make it

1/2 Take a large cereal box for the base and a small box for the cabin and cover both with contrasting gummed paper or plain wallpaper.

3 Take a cardboard kitchen roll tube and paint it in a bright colour. Write on the name of a petrol company with a felt-tipped pen.

4 Make four holes through the cereal box, two at the front and two at the back and push through two thin dowels long enough to hold a cotton reel at each end with 1 cm protruding.

5 Colour the end of each cotton reel with felt-tipped pen and push on to the ends of the dowels. Wind sellotape round as shown to several thicknesses to prevent the cotton reels slipping off.

6 Assemble base, cabin and cardboard tube with strong glue and add shapes from coloured paper for windows and doors and men's faces cut out from old magazines.

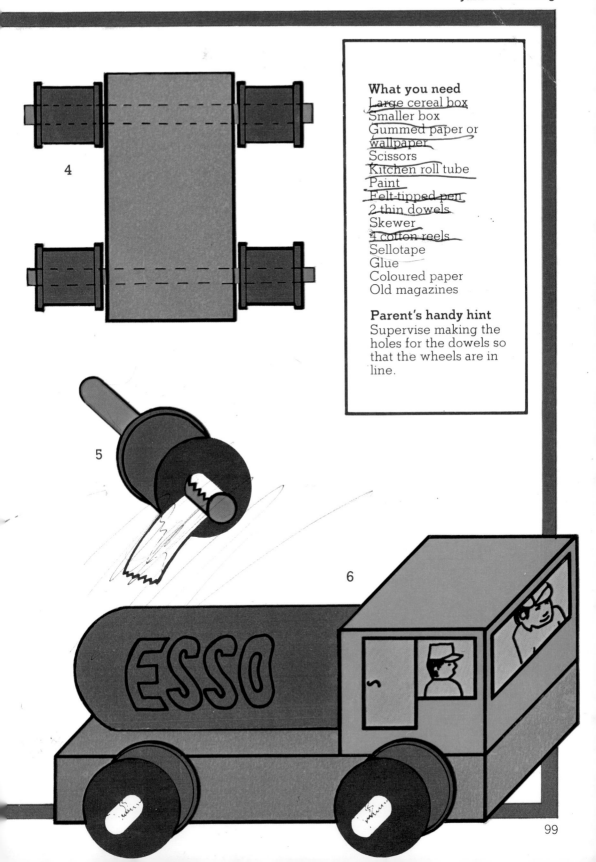

4

What you need
Large cereal box
Smaller box
Gummed paper or
wallpaper
Scissors
Kitchen roll tube
Paint
Felt-tipped pen
2 thin dowels
Skewer
4 cotton reels
Sellotape
Glue
Coloured paper
Old magazines

Parent's handy hint
Supervise making the
holes for the dowels so
that the wheels are in
line.

5

6

ESSO

Circle Quiz

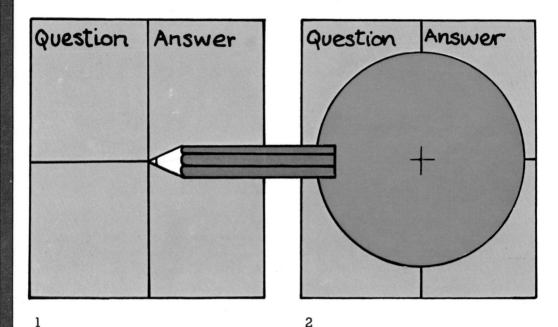

Question	Answer

1

Question	Answer

2

How to make it

1. Take a piece of card approximately 25 cm x 20 cm and find the centre by measuring half way along each side and drawing a line across. Pierce a hole through the centre. Write QUESTION on the left side and ANSWER on the right.

2. From a second piece of card in a different colour draw a circle as large as possible using a plate or a lid as a guide. Cut out the circle and place it on the base card. Pierce a hole through the centre.

3. Cut out the shape shown from the circle and attach the circle to the base card with a paper fastener.

4. Draw around the cut out shape as you turn the circle so that the base card looks as shown. Write the questions and answers in the spaces and colour each pair with the same colour as shown.

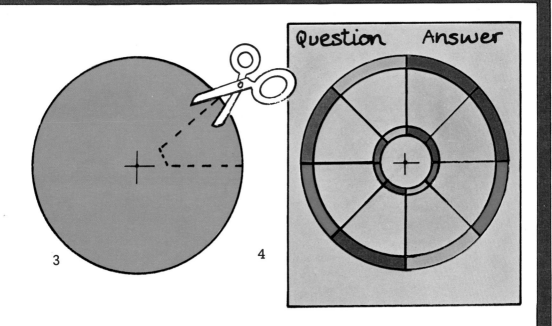

3

4

What you need
2 pieces of card
Ruler
Pencil
Scissors
Plate or lid to draw a
large circle
Skewer
Paper fastener
Crayons

Parent's handy hint
The aim of this simply
made quiz is to
encourage children to
search for information
using reference books
and encyclopaedias.
Younger children will
have fun making up
topical questions relating
to their own interests,
from television, sport and
the pop world.

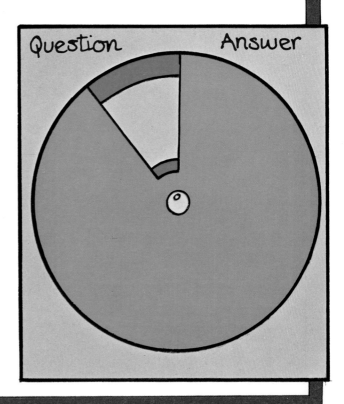

Crafty Mousse Faces

No Bake

How to make them

1. Dissolve the jelly in 150 ml (¼ pint) of boiling water.
2. Grate the rind and squeeze the juice of the lemon and add to the jelly. Leave the jelly to cool but *not* to set.
3. Carefully separate the egg whites from the yolks placing them in separate basins. Whisk the yolks with the sugar until the mixture is light and creamy.
4. When the jelly is cool, add the yolks and mix together thoroughly.
5. Clean the whisk and then whip the egg whites before folding the mixture into the jelly. Spoon the mixture into individual dishes and leave in the fridge to set.
6. To add the faces use chocolate polka dots or buttons for eyes, and a glacé cherry for a nose, pieces of orange for a mouth and eyebrows and grated chocolate for hair.

3

6

5

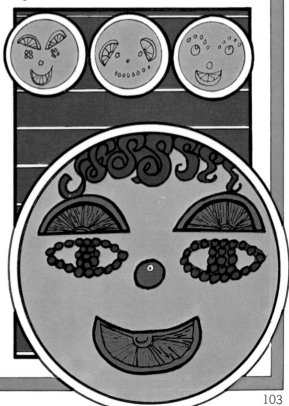

Chocolate Biscuit Cakes

No Bake

How to make them
1. Beat the butter and the syrup together in the bowl.
2. Crush the biscuits with a rolling pin.
3. Add the biscuits to the bowl together with the milk and drinking chocolate and mix together.
4. Form small balls of the mixture and place in waxed sweet cases.

2

What you need
Large bowl
Wooden spoon
Rolling pin
Pastry board
Waxed sweet cases
Knob of butter
1 tablespoon of golden syrup
100 g (4 oz) of sweet biscuits
1 tablespoon drinking chocolate
1 tablespoon milk

Parent's handy hint
The best tools for dividing mixtures are hands and fingers. Discuss the importance of cleanliness to avoid germs and infection.

4

Uncle Sam's Banana Whizz

No Bake

How to make it

1 Cut the banana in half length-
   ways and place the two halves
   together on a dish.
2 Put the two scoops of ice cream
   between the two halves.
3 Pour the butterscotch sauce on
   the strawberry ice cream and
   the strawberry syrup on the
   chocolate ice cream.
4 Cover with the double cream
   and sprinkle with grated
   chocolate. Top with a fresh
   strawberry.

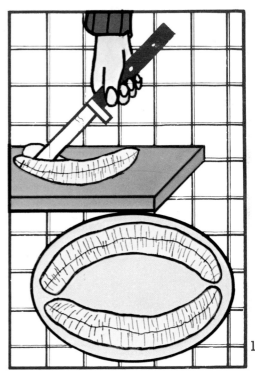

1

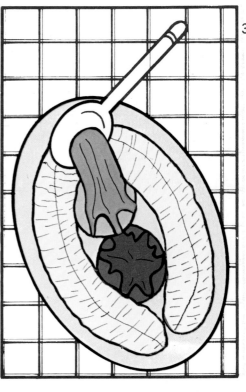

3

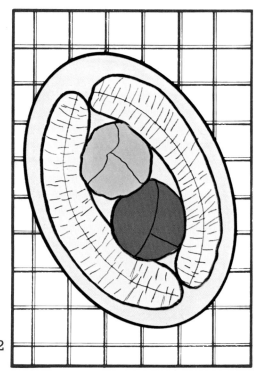

2

What you need
1 large dish
1 large banana
1 scoop chocolate ice cream
1 scoop strawberry ice cream
1 spoonful strawberry syrup
1 spoonful butterscotch sauce
1 tablespoon double cream
Grated chocolate
1 fresh strawberry

Parent's handy hint
An ideal dish to prepare to celebrate the Fourth of July. Discuss the festival (see Introduction).

4

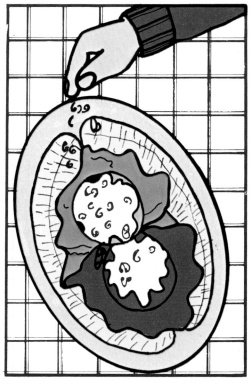

Coconut Barfi

How to make it

1. Bring the milk to boil in a large saucepan and simmer until reduced to about half a litre.
2. Stir in the cocount, cardamom seeds and sugar and continue cooking until thick, stirring all the time.
3. Pour half the mixture into a shallow, greased dish. Add a few drops of pink colouring to the remainder and stir well.
4. Pour the remainder into a second greased dish and leave both to set.
5. When cool, cut the mixture into small squares.

1

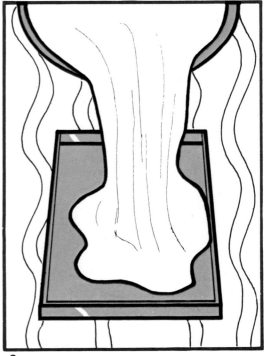

3

2

What you need
Large saucepan
Wooden spoon
2 shallow dishes
100 g (4 oz) dessicated coconut
75 g (3 oz) sugar
1 litre (2 pints) milk
2 cardamom seeds (crushed)
Pink colouring

Parent's handy hint
Supervise the stirring of the hot liquid for the small child. This is a traditional Indian sweet which is very popular at festivals.

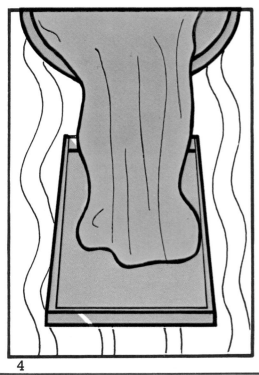

4

5

Turkey Tasters

1

How to make them

1 Make up the parsley sauce in the bowl according to the directions on the packet and add the minced turkey, the egg yolk and seasoning. Mix well and leave to get cold.
2 Roll the mixture into small balls.
3 Beat up the egg white and dip the balls into it and then roll each in the breadcrumbs.
4 Carefully heat a pan of deep fat and lower the balls in a frying basket into the hot fat. Fry until brown and crispy, drain well on kitchen paper and serve hot on cocktail sticks.

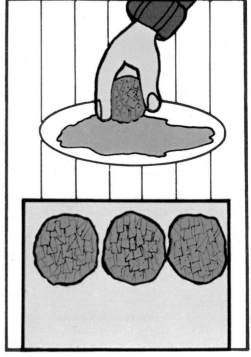
3

What you need
Mixing bowl
Deep pan with frying
basket
Cocktail sticks
1 packet instant parsley
sauce mix
1 egg separated
450 g (1lb) cooked
minced turkey
Salt and pepper
Breadcrumbs

Parent's handy hint
This involves deep frying
in hot fat and this *must*
be done under your
supervision.

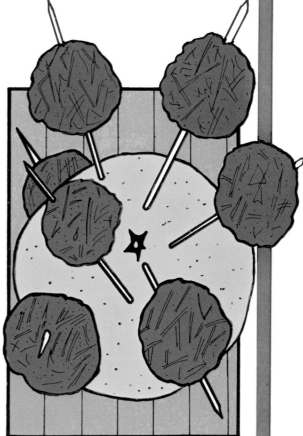

Chanukah Latkes

1

How to make them

1   Grate the potatoes and onion into a bowl.
2   Drain off any excess liquid.
3   Add the flour, eggs and seasoning and stir to a smooth batter.
4   Carefully heat a shallow pan of oil and add spoonfuls of the mixture, turning to brown on both sides.
5   Drain well on kitchen paper and serve hot.

4

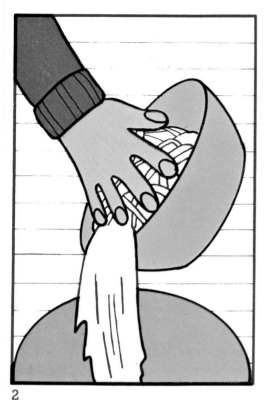

2

3

5

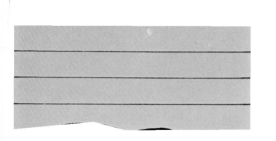

What you need
Mixing bowl
Grater
Frying pan
4 large potatoes
1 small onion
3 tablespoons plain flour
2 small eggs
Salt and pepper

Parent's handy hint
Supervise the heating of
the oil. This is a traditional
Chanukah dish and can
stimulate discussion
about this festival (see
also the Menorah on page
48 and Introduction).

Salami Surprises

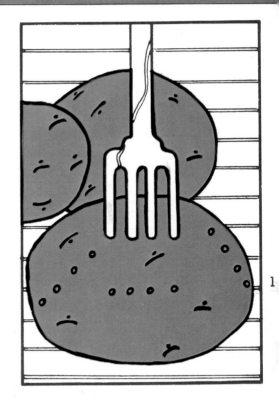

1

How to make them

1   Scrub the potatoes well and prick them all over with a fork.
2   Make three cuts in each potato deep enough to hold a slice of salami in each.
3   Place a slice of salami in each cut and cover each potato with aluminium foil.
4   Bake the potatoes in a medium oven at 375°F (Gas mark 5) for 1¼ hours.
5   Serve each potato wrapped in a serviette and pass around small dishes of relish.

3

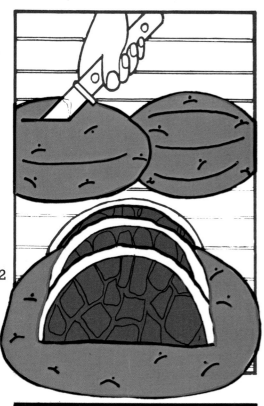

2

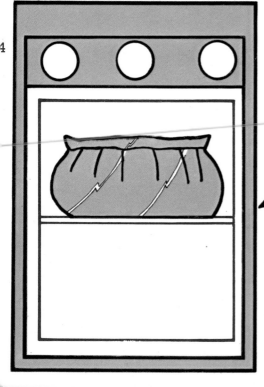

4

What you need
For each person:
1 large potato
3 slices of salami
Dishes of relish
Serviettes

Parent's handy hint
This needs a hot oven
and so supervision is
needed, particularly
when removing the
potatoes when cooked.

5

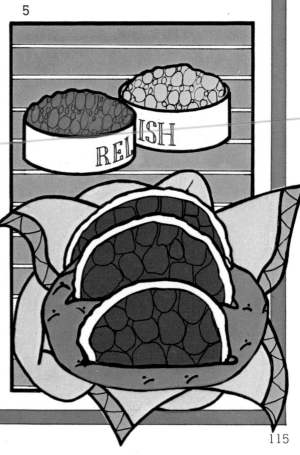

Templates

Christmas Bell

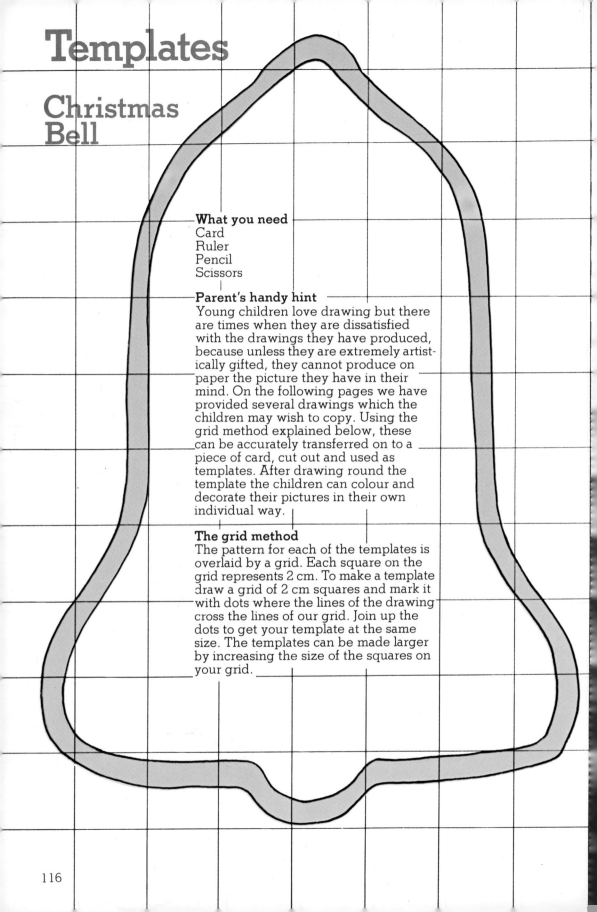

What you need
Card
Ruler
Pencil
Scissors

Parent's handy hint
Young children love drawing but there
are times when they are dissatisfied
with the drawings they have produced,
because unless they are extremely artistically gifted, they cannot produce on
paper the picture they have in their
mind. On the following pages we have
provided several drawings which the
children may wish to copy. Using the
grid method explained below, these
can be accurately transferred on to a
piece of card, cut out and used as
templates. After drawing round the
template the children can colour and
decorate their pictures in their own
individual way.

The grid method
The pattern for each of the templates is
overlaid by a grid. Each square on the
grid represents 2 cm. To make a template
draw a grid of 2 cm squares and mark it
with dots where the lines of the drawing
cross the lines of our grid. Join up the
dots to get your template at the same
size. The templates can be made larger
by increasing the size of the squares on
your grid.

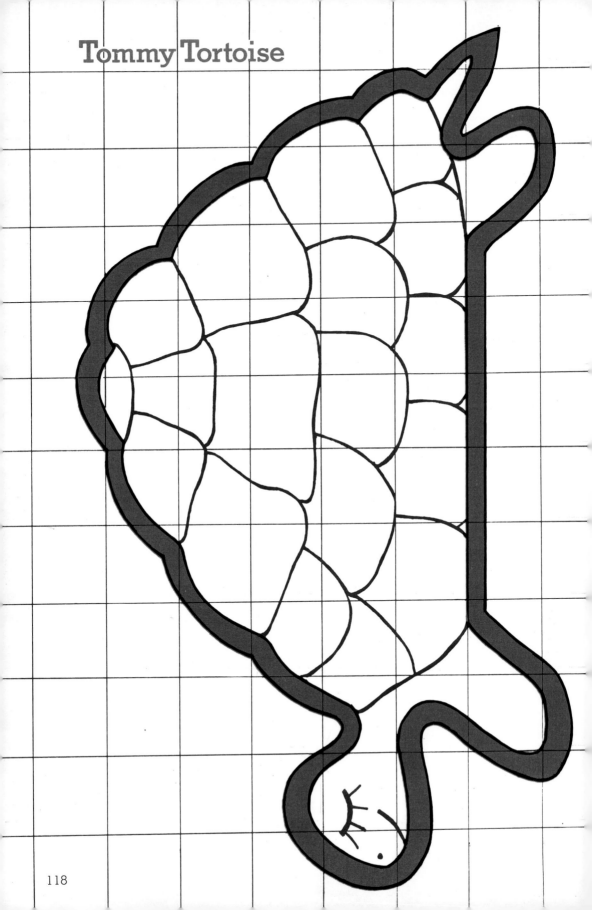

Tommy Tortoise

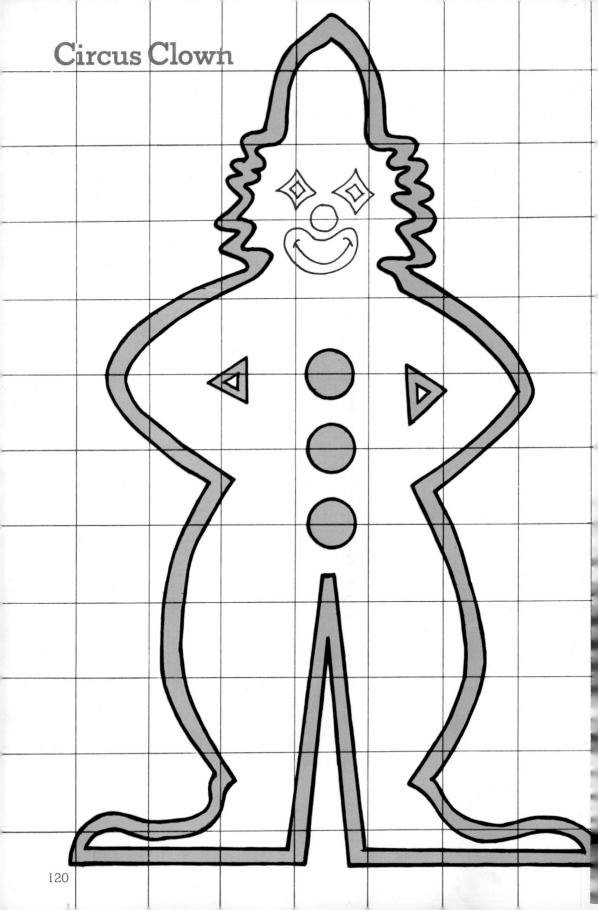

Circus Clown

120

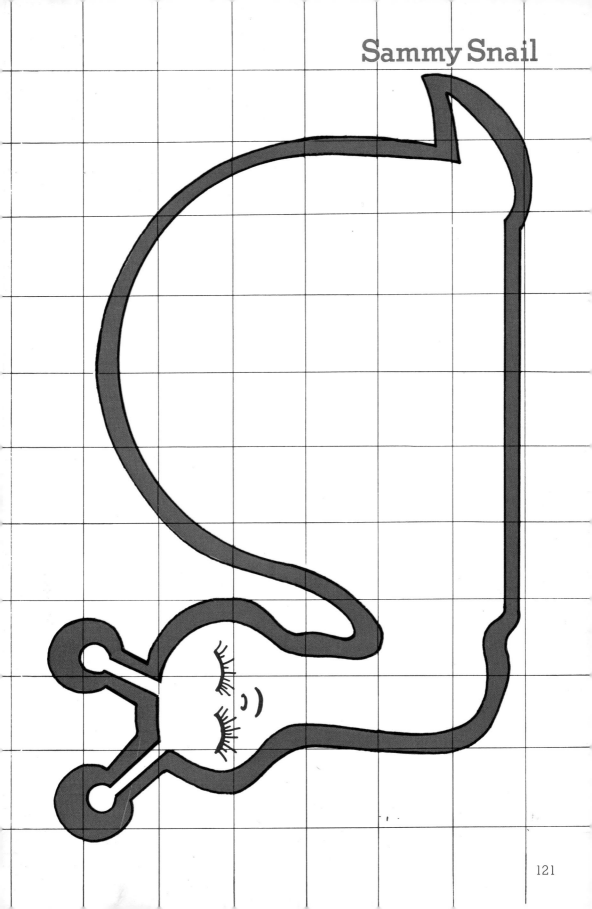

Percy Pixie

122

Mad March Hare

123

Christmas Star

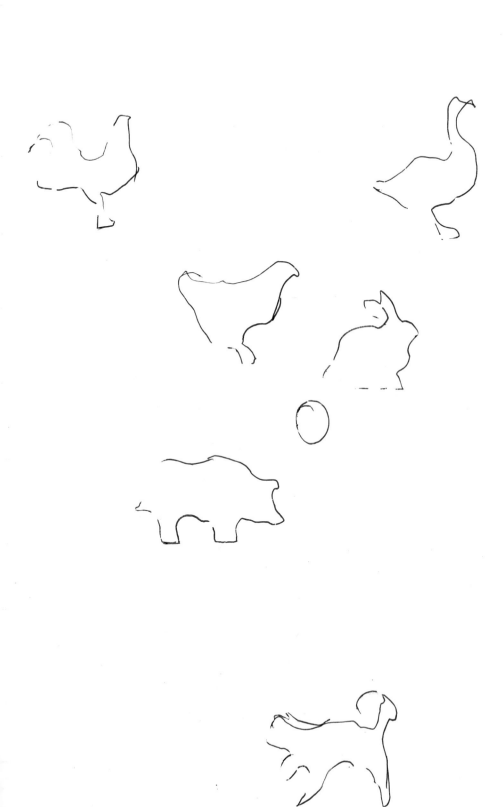